Kairos — Greek term for a moment of truth, a critical and decisive moment, a time of grace and opportunity, a challenge to decision and action.

KAIROS

Confessions of a Gay Priest

Zalmon O.
SHERWOOD

Boston • Alyson Publications

Published as a trade paperback original by
Alyson Publications, 40 Plympton St., Boston, Mass. 02118.
Distributed in the U.K. by GMP Publishers,
PO Box 247, London, N15 6RW, England.

First U.S. edition: April, 1987

ISBN 1-55583-102-8

10 April 1990

To Stephen and Minos

*and to Phil,
who attended my program
at Dignity of Honoring.*

Peace,

Zal Sherwood

foreword

As priests, Zal Sherwood and I are called to be advocates of civil rights and liberties for all suffering, oppressed, harassed and disenfranchised persons. While participating in the civil rights movement for blacks in the 1960s, I realized that gay people suffered similar discrimination and persecution. I also observed how religious institutions would gladly take money, time and talent from gay men and lesbians while condemning their sexual identity and behavior.

One of the most familiar mottos of the Episcopal Church reads, "The Episcopal Church welcomes you." Yes, the Episcopal Church welcomes lesbians and gay men as long as they are discreet (a particularly high virtue in Anglicanism). Despite their attempts to formulate a more enlightened sexual ethic, many religious leaders still believe that the only good sex occurs in heterosexual marriage. According to such leaders, all other sex (homosexual, pre-nuptial, extra-marital, post-marital, masturbation) is sinful.

At Trinity Church, we work toward an attitude of positive sex. I encourage my parishioners to enjoy their sexuality. Much of my pastoral counseling deals with sexual issues. During my thirty years as a priest, I have observed how frequently a person's spiritual problems relate to her or his sexual problems. People have lousy sex, no sex, frightened, guilty sex — sex that is neither satisfying nor wholesome.

During the past five years, I have focused my ministry on single persons (unmarried, divorced, widowed, gay men and lesbians). According to traditional religious teaching, these single persons should deny themselves sex. For eleven years, I was a single man between marriages, during which time I shared a full and active sex life with women. To call such behavior sinful is medieval madness thrust upon the twentieth century. Single persons have at least one thing in common with married couples — we share the same kind of tender, sweet, gentle, aggressive, fleeting, committed, sad, scary, delicious sex. To deny the existence and wholesomeness (and holiness) of single sex is to deny God's presence wherever love is found.

The Episcopal Church is sex negative and hypocritical in its practice of refusing to recognize and affirm the varieties of sexual expression among its clergy and laity. Church officials simply do not want to hear about the meaningful relationships of single Church members. "Oh, it's all right for gays and singles to have sex," some pseudo-liberal Church folk will concede, "as long as they don't flaunt it." More and more people, realizing that their sexual relationships are integral parts of their spiritual formation, are refusing to be discreet any longer, breaking silence and "flaunting it."

The Rev. Zalmon O. Sherwood has discovered the cost of coming out as a gay priest. This is a book of letters to his friend, Stephen, a former seminary classmate who currently works as a writer and teacher in Athens, Greece. The letters were written during the period between Zal's graduation from seminary and his resignation seventeen months later as a priest at Emmanuel Episcopal Church, Southern Pines, North Carolina, following the public disclosure of his homosexuality. In the letters, he does not attempt to imitate the style of the Apostle Paul or Jesus. They are simply a subjective, poignant, inspiring chronicle of one gay man's experience of religion, relationships and the affluent South.

Zal's story is not new. I have known hundreds of gay and lesbian priests. They have been excellent pastors, preachers, teachers and counselors, yet they have usually not had the chance to be truly open and honest about the most intimate parts of their lives, i.e., their lovers. If a gay person wants to be ordained and find parish work in the Episcopal Church, that person is, more often than not, forced to hide from fear of exposure, to lie about her or his life by denying the existence of significant relationships and sexual activity.

The ordination of avowed, practicing lesbians and gay men is essential for an honest, effective ministry in religious institutions. Such a move would pave the way for all people, homosexual and heterosexual, to be free and positive about their sexuality. If religious leaders were more at ease with their sexuality, they would be better qualified to assist their parishioners in integrating their sexuality with their spirituality.

The Episcopal Church and other religious institutions make a big deal about treating lesbian and gay persons as 'children of God,' yet religious leaders continue to duck the issues in facing the ordination of open homosexuals and the blessing and marriage of homosexual relationships. The Episcopal Church has most recently joined the media, the Congress and the medical profession in focusing on AIDS, but it does little to alleviate sex prejudice against gay people in our society and religious institutions. Religious leaders are content to focus on an illness — AIDS — and they continue to patronize gay people by offering help only to the sick while refusing to publicly support the healthy. The Church itself will continue to be sick and unhealthy, broken and forsaken, until it recognizes lesbians and gay men as human equals, worthy of all sacraments.

The Rev. Robert Warren Cromey
Rector
Trinity Episcopal Church
San Francisco, California

author's note

Pastoral confidentiality is essential to the priestly vocation, for a pastor is often privy to the most intimate parts of people's lives, and is expected to keep his or her mouth shut about such confessions. Episcopalians share with Roman Catholics the belief that confession is a sacrament and whatever is discussed between a priest and a parishioner is sacrosanct and can go no further. Colleagues will criticize me for writing candidly about various aspects of my ministry, but I have changed names, and where appropriate, circumstances to protect the confidence of certain parishioners. All other names and incidents remain intact.

I have also chosen not to expose the names of closeted gay seminary professors, priests, monks, archdeacons, cathedral deans and bishops who have made sexual advances toward me since I began the ordination process. Coming out publicly as a gay priest was neither a foolish nor courageous act; it was simply my way of responding to the cumulative sexual harassment and discrimination I experienced from the Episcopal dioceses of Ohio, Massachusetts and North Carolina.

Liberation is never theoretical. It's based on the heart, and it arises out of a critically examined, lived experience of oppression, above all, of the personal fight to assert one's dignity. The most important front of that fight, the one with one's own self, I've already won. There is no turning back.

The Rev. Zalmon O. Sherwood
Santa Fe, New Mexico
Easter Day, 1986

the Ordination

The bishop addresses the ordinand as follows:

My brother (or sister), the Church is the family of God, the body of Christ, and the temple of the Holy Spirit. All baptized people are called to make Christ known as Savior and Lord, and to share in the renewing of His world. Now you are called to work as pastor, priest, and teacher, together with your bishop and fellow presbyters, and to take your share in the councils of the Church.

As a priest, it will be your task to proclaim by word and deed the Gospel of Jesus Christ, and to fashion your life in accordance with its precepts. You are to love and serve the people among whom you work, caring alike for young and old, strong and weak, rich and poor. You are to preach, to declare God's forgiveness to penitent sinners, to pronounce God's blessing, to share in the administration of Holy Baptism and in the celebration of the mysteries of

Christ's Body and Blood, and to perform the other ministrations entrusted to you.

In all that you do, you are to nourish Christ's people from the riches of His grace, and strengthen them to glorify God in this life and in the life to come.

My brother (or sister), do you believe that you are truly called by God and His Church to this priesthood?

Answer: I believe I am so called.

Do you now in the presence of the Church commit yourself to this trust and responsibility?

Answer: I do.

Will you respect and be guided by the pastoral direction and leadership of your bishop?

Answer: I will.

Will you be diligent in reading and study of the Holy Scriptures, and in seeking the knowledge of such things as may make you a stronger and more able minister of Christ?

Answer: I will.

Will you endeavor so to minister the Word of God and the sacraments of the New Covenant, that the reconciling love of Christ may be known and received?

Answer: I will.

Will you undertake to be a faithful pastor to all whom you are called to serve, laboring together with them and with your fellow ministers to build up the family of God?

Answer: I will.

Will you do your best to pattern your life in accordance with the teachings of Christ, so that you may be a wholesome example to your people?

Answer: I will.

Will you persevere in prayer, both in public and in private, asking God's grace, both for yourself and for others, offering all your labors to God, through the mediation of Jesus Christ, and in the sanctification of the Holy Spirit?

Answer: I will.

May the Lord who has given you the will to do these things give you the grace and power to perform them.

Answer: Amen.

— from The Ordination of a Priest,
The Book of Common Prayer

KAIROS

Cambridge, MA
May 23, 1984

Dear Stephen,

Just two days until commencement! I remember how splendid your Harvard ceremony was last year, and how proud I was to know the most brilliant (and handsome) member of the Divinity School class. Walking home that afternoon, I began crying, because I selfishly didn't want you to leave Cambridge and move so far away. How would I survive my final year of seminary without you? (And it hasn't been easy.) Who would be my lane partner at Blodgett Pool? What would the future hold for you in Greece? How could the Episcopal Church, our Church, refuse to ordain such an extraordinarily gifted candidate as yourself to the priesthood?

I've been busy packing my books and music in boxes, and sending them off to North Carolina. Last night I ran across the book of Cavafy poems which you gave me. Do you know his poem, 'Perilous Things'?

> Fortified by theory and study,
> I shall not fear my passions like a coward.
> I shall yield my body to sensual delights,
> to enjoyments that one dreams about,
> to the most audacious amorous desires,

> to the wanton impulses of the blood,
> without
> a single fear, for whatever I wish—
> and I shall have the will, fortified
> as I shall be by theory and by study—
> at moments of crisis, I shall find again
> my spirit, as before, ascetic.

The poem describes us well, no? Or, how about these lines from 'The Souls of Old Men' which could serve as a tribute to many bishops we know:

> In their bodies wasted and aged
> sit the souls of old men. . .
> the confounded and contradictory
> souls, that sit — comicotragical—
> In their aged worn-out hides.

You will be relieved to learn that the Provincetown weekend with Mark was less stormy than I anticipated. For the first time in months, he was serious about communicating with me. He doesn't want me to leave. He keeps telling me to stop before it's too late, that the Church is an oppressive, unhealthy institution for gay persons, that I need to reconsider ordination, continue my musical career and remain in relationship with him.

Of course none of our friends are speaking to me because I have chosen to leave him. I hate being criticized by peers for dating so many different men. All of us have friends who have been diagnosed with AIDS, and the fear is that the more men I sleep with, the greater the risk of my contracting the disease. Also, there is this pervading, moralistic view at seminary that we gay persons should work toward committing ourselves to a single, mono-

gamous relationship, so that we might be 'good role
models' for other gays. While I am the first to uphold and
celebrate long-term, committed relationships among my
heterosexual, bisexual and homosexual friends, I also
believe that my various short-term relationships with men
contain elements of tenderness, honesty, grace and
redemption. I wish I could remain with the same lover
forever, because that is the norm, the ideal which Christian ethics recommends. When I hear couples describe the
depth of their spirituality, their intimacy and trust, I say,
"Yes, that's what I want." Still, it hasn't happened for me,
and I must accept responsibility for my reluctance, my
failure to commit myself to one man for life. I shall
continue to love men who understand and respect my
limitations, my need to be available to other men and
women, my commitment to my priestly duties and
music.

Still, none of our friends can understand why I need
the chance to use my education and exercise my ministry,
alone and far away from Mark. I'm not sure I even understand. Did I tell you over the phone that Mark had
explored the possibility of moving his practice to Pinehurst in order to be near me? He keeps saying how weary
he is of Boston winters and how the South has always
appealed to him. But I need at least one year away from
him, so now he has arranged to spend the year in Vienna
doing research — just think, you will be closer to Mark
than I. Lucky you!

Isn't it strange that you and I never approved of each
other's lovers? As painful as it was for you, I was so glad
when you finally decided to break up with that pompous
ass of a lawyer. How could you ever have loved a man
who was so hostile toward me, your best friend? At least

Mark enjoyed you; indeed, I'm sure he lusted for you. You always dismissed him as a bore, a gorgeous bore, but a bore nevertheless. And as you pointed out, I was probably more in love with his Beacon Hill brownstone, his Provincetown condominium, his Porsche, his wardrobe and his body than I ever was with Mark, the man. We have so little in common, so little to discuss, almost no feelings to share other than sex, but at least last weekend was a beginning. He truly started talking to me as his lover instead of simply one of his patients. And now we have agreed to separate for a year. I should be happy, right? As always, I have gotten what I wanted from him, yet I can't help feeling that I am making a terrible mistake by leaving him. He is certain to take a lover in Vienna, and our trial separation may become permanent.

Why can't you be here when I need you? I tried calling you a few minutes ago, but again there was no answer. You're never at home, even when I call you at 3 a.m. Athens time. You must be seeing someone. Why don't you write me something about him? I can't help but be concerned about you. Your letters reveal how lonely and exhausted you are, so different from the Stephen I remember. If you were here now, we would go dancing late into the night, then retire to that wonderful deli near the Fenway for cheesecake and coffee. We wouldn't stop talking until sunrise, when the waitress would appear and take our breakfast orders.

I'm ready to leave Cambridge. For the past year I have been living off memories of time spent with you; sitting together in class and passing notes about a particularly attractive professor; walking along the Charles riverbank to Blodgett Pool for our daily workouts; napping beneath

the lilacs in the Longfellow Garden; rehearsing the Bach
violin sonatas late at night in the chapel. I've missed
laughing with you and crying with you. How many times
would I appear at your door in tears, only to be greeted
with a kleenex box while you sat quietly beside me, your
soft green eyes and silent prayers focused on me? I cried
about a suicidal lover, rejection by family and friends, an
abusive bishop. You challenged me to grieve, to explore
my feelings in creative ways that have made me aware of
a greater power within myself.

Today I still grieve for you, Stephen, because I have
witnessed the sensitivity, integrity and power of your
priestly vocation. When we volunteered at the Boston
halfway house, I would watch you relate pastorally to
homeless gay youths, jobless gay adults, battered women,
poor and hungry persons. You taught me to take seriously
God's call to serve the poor, to draw on my experience as
a gay man in order to serve persons who also find
themselves at the margins of society. Despite your good
looks, you taught me that being gay is not pretty. While I
would react in horror, you would embrace a bleeding
victim of a queerbashing incident. While I would dwell on
my mortality, you would offer love and compassion to an
emaciated AIDS patient. While I would lobby peacefully
for gay rights legislation, you would organize a sit-in at
the governor's office and spend time in jail for demanding
equal rights for lesbians and gay men.

For the past four years, I have been consumed with
coursework, papers and deadlines, exams, forums,
committee meetings, work-study, rehearsals, perform-
ances and services, and fitting in all that I must do, and
all that I must learn. I attended seminary because it was

clear to me that here was a critical place where people studied, prayed and took action against injustice. Cambridge and Boston offered me some of the best opportunities for a theological and musical education.

As I approach commencement, I am more aware of my limitations, of what I can and cannot give, about when to say "yes" and when to say "no". I am more able now to let go of personal illusions about myself and cultural illusions about homosexuality and how I, as a gay man, am to act. I know now that when I am clear about who I am and am able to affirm the truth about myself, there is a better chance that I will be able to share myself with others in ways that are more honest, believable and trustworthy.

It has been difficult for us, as gay men seeking ordination in the Episcopal Church, to find the support needed for substantial growth in vocational, professional and personal formation. We have suffered rampant discrimination from seminary and diocesan officials. Certain faculty members, bishops, clergy and so-called spiritual directors have exhibited homophobic tendencies that can only be described as manipulative, unconscionable and anti-Christian.

These ecclesiastical authorities will go so far as to admit that I need not feel guilty about my homosexuality, but in the same breath they discourage me from integrating and expressing it as part of my spiritual life. They are eager to validate my skills as a seminarian and musician as long as I do not reveal and share parts of my inner life which focus on my relationship with Mark. In their heartless attempts to conceal and repress my sexuality, in their condescending commandment to hate the sin but love the sinner, in their alarming, repugnant moves to sexually seduce and harass me into duplicity and silence, in their prejudicial refusal to allow me to speak publicly on issues of human sexuality from my gay perspective, they are sabotaging principles of academic and religious freedom, smothering my soul and banishing me to a spiritual wasteland.

Does this mean, as Church leaders tell me, that I have an authority problem, that I set standards too high for those I expect to teach and advise me, that I expect in four years time, faculty and bishops should also grow into more honest, accepting, thoughtful human beings? Seeking ordination seems like an impossible task when you consider the discouraging signals from religious homophobes in our respective dioceses. But I attended seminary for other reasons: to study theology, to learn about the history of minorities, to reclaim and reform a part of my faith which had been shattered by institutional prejudice, bigotry and hypocrisy of Church and society; and most important of all, to learn to rely on my lesbian and gay friends, to form relationships, to create bonds that empower me to confront and disarm the dehumanizing evils of homophobia and heterosexism.

I believe gay men and lesbians can fill a gap in the quality of ministry in the Church — we can bring talent and sensitivity to the profession.

As you have always said, Stephen, there are a lot of folks out there who need people like us. They need me not to worry about one decision or another; they need me not to complain about an exam grade or a mediocre recital; they need me to open my eyes and my ears and my heart to them, to reach out and minister to their needs. In life, one doesn't get many exam grades and musical jury marks. It is, after all, what I think of my

own self, my relationship with God and humanity, that
matter So I'm leaning toward ordination, and praying that
it is available to me, and I to it.

With my love,
Zal

❧

Southern Pines, NC
June 7, 1984

Dear Stephen,

Mark surprised me by attending commencement! He
is so anti-Church it was strange to see him actually
worshipping something other than the medical profession.
I was relieved to notice an older woman assisting him
through the service; otherwise, he would have been
completely lost! After the ceremony, he helped me pack a
few last-minute things, then sent me on my way in my
Toyota.

I made the mistake of spending the first night with
my youngest sister, Dorothy, in Philadelphia. Remember
the monthly letters she would send me, the ones in which
she wrote how I was attending the wrong seminary (too
liberal by her standards), that because I am gay, I had no
business even being at seminary, that unless I would
repent and follow Jesus, I would burn in Hell? And all this
from my sister, the cardiologist! Because she is closest in
age to me, I have always confided much to her. She and
her husband, Peter, have always been gracious to me,
even though we tend to disagree on both theological and
ethical matters.

This last visit was no exception. I hadn't been at their
house fifteen minutes when suddenly I found myself in

the midst of an impromptu Bible study. This on the day
of my graduation from seminary! As committed, born-
again Christians, Dorothy and Peter disapprove of my gay
lifestyle and feel that if Christ were first in my life, I
would be able to repress my sexual needs. They believe in.
basing all their actions on Scripture. No matter what the
familiar biblical passages proscribe concerning human
sexuality, I believe the subject is too complex and
mysterious to be able to outline God's intentions and
boundaries with my sister and brother-in-law's apparent
ease.

   /   My sexuality is a gift from God, who calls me into
relationship with other men. Christian tradition defines
God as 'Trinity,' or mutuality, communion and vulner-
ability. No other religion, therefore, provides such a basis
for a theology of relationship, a sexual and spiritual
yearning for relationships which are liberating, honest,
faithful, socially responsible and joyous. God is not a
passionless, omnipotent loner who depends on Her own
individual efforts. On the contrary, the Bible reveals God
as angry, tender, jealous, irrepressibly and hopelessly in
love with creation. We will learn how to be properly
sexual as we understand the properly passionate relationship God has with us. And we will become properly
spiritual as we come to understand the divine character of
human longing and affection in our relationships.

      I made the mistake of telling Dorothy and Peter that I
am opposed to taking the Oath of Conformity when I am
ordained to the diaconate at the end of this month.
During the oath, I am expected to state that I believe the
Bible to be 'the Word of God,' but I'm not sure I
understand what that means and therefore cannot pledge
myself to upholding it. Frankly, there is much in the

Bible that I find just plain wrong. When my fundamentalist friends and relatives use the Word of God to prooftext me to the bowels of Hell, I wonder if somehow it might be a more humane, hospitable place than their Heaven. Dorothy and Peter were aghast when I explained to them that for me, God's Word was not some rigid ethical code, but rather, was active, alive and fleshly in the form of Christ and other great biblical, historical and contemporary figures who inspire us, open us to various interpretations of God's mighty acts, depending on our given culture and generation. In the same oath, I am expected to state that I will obey the doctrine, discipline and worship of the Church, but I cannot do this if, in any given situation, they are being used to promote injustice.

Needless to say, I don't expect them to attend my ordination, as they consider me an unworthy candidate for Holy Orders. I can't help but respect their strong faith and convictions, so much that some days I look in the mirror and wonder if indeed I am on the wrong track. Yet I can only trust how God's Spirit acts in my life. I probably will be a wimpy priest because I refuse to judge people or try to impose my values on them. I avoid people who tend to be more rejecting than others, more tentative, "yes, but" people. Only the totally affirming, spontaneous and unreserved can help me in my struggle to discern God's will, and give me the courage and strength to explore new facets of my ministry, to take new risks, to confront life actively.

Many charismatic Christians greatly irk me. I see in their enthusiastic and, frankly, self-serving claims to direct divine revelation, nothing but a frivolous flight from what I consider to be the painful ambiguities of the

Word — such as Jesus on the cross, lesbians and gay men in social limbo, discouraged unemployed fathers killing their children and themselves. All these and countless other incidents seem to disappear beneath charismatics' placid surface of direct, divine experience. God may indeed be doing something for Dorothy and Peter that God has not done for me. When I occasionally say that, it results in pressure to attend the next church revival or, more acceptably, promises of prayers for me.

Continuing my drive south, I stopped and had lunch with Michael in Washington. He still loves his parish work and has recently obtained a grant to open a 24-hour shelter for the homeless. And, he shocked me by announcing his engagement to one of his parishioners, a beautiful woman named Kimberly (he even carries a photograph of her) who is on the staff at the National Gallery and who also happens to be an heir to the DuPont fortune.

So how would you have reacted? I was in the midst of biting into a turkey sandwich when he told me about her. He blushed and turned his head aside, so I hope he didn't notice my incredulous stare. Michael, engaged? Impossible. Yet you would have been proud of me. I quickly pulled myself together, smiled, and asked the waiter to bring us a bottle of champagne. I ended up consuming most of it — Michael had to return to the office for a 2 p.m. appointment, but not before asking me to arrange the music and to serve as best man for the wedding, which will be held at his parish in mid-September.

I immediately agreed to do both, even though I have serious misgivings about this proposed marriage. Michael says he wants to have children. We are told that success lies in getting married and having children. When we reach a certain age and still haven't married, we begin to suffer much rejection and ostracism from pro-family persons and institutions. You and I both know that Michael is ambitious enough to become a bishop someday, and I find myself wondering how long Kimberly will be in the picture if she doesn't obtain a mitre for him sometime in the next twenty years. It hurts me to have a man with whom I have made love suddenly decide he wants to marry a woman. I'm trying so hard to understand, to accept this situation with joy and serenity. It is wrong of me to place Michael in the exclusively gay category. Perhaps he is bisexual, or truly heterosexual, but you and I know that such a change, in Michael's case, would truly be miraculous.

I arrived late that night at my parents' house, where your letter was waiting for me. They live in a posh retirement village about thirty miles west of Southern Pines. It has always been difficult for me to be with my parents, and now we are practically neighbors. For many reasons, I did not see myself working in the golf capital of the nation, or beginning my ministry so near my parents, but the Southern Pines position was the only job available to me. Ohio and New England parishes which were aware of my gay rights activity would not touch me with a ten-foot pole. During my Southern Pines interview, the gay issue never arose. The search committee at Emmanuel Church wanted a young minister who could develop strong music and youth programs, so I was hired. Unlike the Roman Catholic Church, the Episcopal Church has a surfeit of clergy with too few positions available for seminary graduates. Women and gays are usually among the last to find parish jobs. Everyone tells me that I should be grateful to have been hired by Emmanuel Church, and while I am looking forward to working as an assistant minister and music director, I'm not sure that I feel all that grateful, but rather curious as to why God has called me to begin my ministry in the middle of North Carolina, in one of the most conservative, affluent resort areas of the country. Perhaps all my experience as a country club brat will finally come in handy.

People have been very kind in welcoming me to Southern Pines. I'm renting a small grey house near the church. Parishioners have been stopping by to leave gifts of cookies, cheese and wine. One of the Church women's guilds held a curate's 'shower' for me, during which I received household gifts — tableware, kitchenware, appliances, towels and linens. Fortunately I haven't had to do any cooking, as people have graciously invited me to their homes for dinner. I love spending time in their homes (most of which are large and elegant), hearing all about their lives, admiring their various collections and handiwork, sitting through countless carousels of family slides. The only thing I don't like is when they start telling me about their eligible young daughters. How do I tactfully explain that it is their sons whom I would enjoy meeting?

I'm off to Cleveland for a final battery of examinations, a pre-ordination retreat, and then, God willing and the people consenting, the ordination itself.

With my love,
Zal

ଈ

Cedar Hills, OH
June 29, 1984

Dear Stephen,

It is the eve of my ordination, and I am spending a sleepless night in a log cabin in the middle of the woods of our diocesan camp in Ohio. I've just returned from a long walk along the riverbank. The river here is not calm like the Charles, but turbulent, twisting and winding with rapids and waterfalls. Like me, the river absorbs much of what it touches in the course of its wanderings. Twenty-seven miles — or 27 years — downstream and the river's and my identity are all confused. Our actual nature is obscured by a variety of additives. Mechanisms for cleansing must be found and applied. What is good about God's creation is that beauty is all around us. It merely has to be looked for, uncovered, recognized and believed in.

After my walk, I went skinny-dipping in the camp swimming pool, and I must have awakened one of the nun caretakers. God only knows how long the middle-aged nun, dressed in a nightgown, had been standing on the patio while watching me swim laps in the buff. I noticed her standing aghast during my first rest period, and she immediately began chastising me for swimming alone in the middle of the night. Perhaps there is a reason to be ordained, so that nuns will no longer yell at me.

Despite all this nocturnal activity, I still can't sleep, because like my sister, Dorothy, and my former lover, Mark, I'm wondering if indeed I am making a mistake by presenting myself tomorrow morning for ordination. I wish I could write that it was excitement that was keeping me awake tonight; rather, everything surrounding my ordination seems contrived and anti-climactic. In other words, I'm suddenly feeling that it simply isn't worth it to be ordained a deacon. Perhaps if your bishop would have agreed to ordain you, I would aspire more to Holy Orders. I don't want to go through with it, Stephen. I wanted to withdraw from the process a year ago, but you have insisted that I submit to ordination. So I'm doing it for you, not for God, not for me, but for Stephen, because you keep telling me how much the Church needs people like us, it needs our witness, and my witness will be more effective as a priest.

When the bishop lays his hands on my head tomorrow, when I speak the oaths and vows which trouble me, I shall, by my access to ordination, become an oppressor of you and other gay persons who are denied ordination. Of course we know that there are gay persons, even avowed gay persons, who are ordained to the ministry. But for reasons I fail to understand, your diocese rejected you, my best friend, as a candidate for the priesthood, and I have made it this far only, in the words of one of the bishop's closeted assistants, "by the skin of my teeth." I've learned, Stephen, that ordination has nothing to do with how fine our credentials are, how well we performed on our comprehensive examinations, how thorough our field work was, how poised, sensitive and articulate we were during endless committee meetings and psychological examinations.

I shall be ordained tomorrow only because my old, homophobic bishop retired in the nick of time, and one of my seminary professors happens to be a good friend of the new, young homophobic bishop. In other words, my professor has persuaded my Ohio bishop, James Moodey, to ordain me, even though there are many in the diocese who are opposed to my ordination on account of my homosexuality. I guess you could call it 'ordination by connection' instead of vocation or accomplishment. I despise the 'old-boy' network and it hurts me to think that I would never have been ordained had it not been for the intervention of my professor.

The entire process leading up to ordination has been so dehumanizing for us gay persons. I knew I wanted to be an Episcopal priest at age 13, which was the same year I discovered my sexual orientation as a gay teenager. I never considered that I might encounter difficulty as a gay candidate for Holy Orders, as my parish priest was gay and a source of spiritual, emotional and vocational support for me as I grew up in a small, agricultural community in Ohio.

Probably the best thing I remember about the parish of my youth is that its red doors were always open. At any hour of the day or night I was able to enter the small church where I would often find others kneeling in prayer, sitting silently, crying or napping. During certain nights, when my parents would become inordinately upset about their only son's homosexuality, I would opt to leave the house for the sanctuary of a pew. By the time I would arrive, certain pews were already occupied by local drunks, railroad bums and Puerto Rican migrant workers.

One frosty November night, at age 16, I had sex in a darkened corner of the church with a migrant worker in his early twenties. We met the next three nights during which I brought him food, warm clothing and money, all of which I, as the son of a surgeon, had in abundance. Then, on the fourth night we were supposed to meet, he never appeared. Still, church remained for me a place where the doors were always open, where I could find peace, love and acceptance, where I could learn about Christ and model my life according to his commandment to love God and to love my neighbor as myself.

Last week I had my final examination by the diocesan psychiatrist. I suppose I took too much initiative in volunteering information under the theory that the psychiatrist would want honesty and frankness. This volunteering made the psychiatrist rather suspicious of me (perhaps justifiably). One problem with these exams is a real confusion between the psychiatrist and the bishop as to what is being examined for. My particular psychiatrist seems to work from an entirely cultural profile of what it would take to be a 'successful' priest (sort of like the optimum funeral director), and some bishops seem to have harbored the notion that the psychiatric exam is primarily a dressed-up lie detector to ferret out trouble in advance (with the bishop and key lay persons acting like suspicious police sergeants, and just about as crude and ignorant). There have been horror stories of shock tactics centered on psychiatric techniques of embarrassment and degradation. One psychiatrist used to insist on the candidate being completely nude. The story is that one candidate quietly complied and then coolly observed, "Enjoying the view, doctor?"

My psychiatrist didn't seem at all interested in the therapist I had been seeing this past year. I've benefited greatly from psychological counseling at seminary, and I plan to continue therapy in North Carolina. Professional counseling is an essential part of the healing and strengthening process, particularly for those who are themselves ministers and ministers-in-training. Therapy has helped me cast off heterosexist societal expectations so that I am able to claim my worth and power as a gay man. In

Cambridge, I was fortunate in having some of the best psychiatric help available in the country, in an environment that understood my intellectual and spiritual needs. In another age, in another type of extended family, perhaps one of my sisters or parents or family friend or priest or peer or lover would be able to help me more as I struggle to understand myself and the world around me. In the absence of all those support networks (with the exception of your letters), I believe I am doing the best possible thing in seeking professional therapy.

My retreat these past few days at the diocesan camp has been therapeutic. The camp is located in a picturesque region of Ohio, with rolling hills and valleys, a countryside quilted with vineyards, corn and soybean fields, small patches of woods, streams, a lake and the river. I've spent most of my time in solitude, praying, reading, writing in my journal, taking long walks. But late last night Elizabeth and Philip, two friends from high school, arrived unannounced at the cabin. Security is so tight at this camp that I'm amazed they were able to sneak past the nuns. We sat drinking wine and reminisced for hours.

Thank you for your beautiful card and icon, marking the occasion of this ordination. In your note, you quoted Keats, "A poet has no identity. He is continually . . . filling some other Body." Perhaps that is the minister's identity, to know himself by continually empathizing with a whole range of life. I shall submit to ordination tomorrow, because you want me to, and because I consider it worth devoting my best gifts and my whole life to becoming a priest who communicates the Spirit of God in my relationships with others, in my celebration

and sharing of the sacraments, in my music and
preaching.

We are young, and in some ways, unripened by
experience. Yet, in other ways, we are seasoned by
experience of which the Church needs now. God has been
working to bring me to accepting who I am, and to
recognize my experience, all my experience but especially
my experience as a gay man, situated at what one might
call the margin of society — the experience of exile — not
as something to be excluded from my ministry but as
vital and integral to it.

My experience of exile informs my vision of what the
Church ought to be and how it should speak of love of
God and neighbor; it provides the means for me to reach
out to people of color, victims of economic and social
injustice, victims of domestic violence, in short, those
also marginalized, with whom I have a common bridge of
experience. I most heartily believe that God has shaped
me for a ministry that includes a commission to lend my
voice to a prophetic critique of the Church's failure to
embrace those at the margins of society as full and central
members of the community of God's people.

My call to the ordained ministry was mediated
through the living encounter with persons who evoked in
me gifts of ministry, of attentive listening, the willingness
to suffer together with another person in need, the
willingness to touch and make love. I refuse to hide my
own brokenness in some darkened sanctuary, or to deny
those aspects of my particular experience which could
most nourish my ministry. The influences upon my
pastoral formation have been many and varied, with yours
being one of the most significant. All of them I carry with

me. I hope that I may continue to listen to their voices and probe their hearts. Yet it is God's music in me that I must sing. It is all that I have to give; anything else rings hollow.

With my love,
Zal

🕸

Southern Pines, NC
July 16, 1984

Dear Stephen,

The phone was ringing when I walked into my house after returning from Ohio, and it was you calling to ask about the ordination. I'm sorry it has taken me over two weeks to write and thank you for your thoughtfulness. I've been busy adjusting to life as a deacon in the Sandhills of North Carolina.

I finally fell asleep after writing you the night before the ordination, and I woke so late in the morning that I thought I would miss the service. By the time I arrived at the vesting room, all my presenters were gathered waiting for me. I had not seen many of them since starting seminary — my sponsoring priest (an older, closeted gay priest from Ohio), a kind vestryman and youth leader from my Ohio parish, a blind woman friend, a musician friend, and a woman priest. They helped me fasten my clerical collar and vested me, and before I knew it, we were processing into the cathedral. It had been four years since I had seen most of my Ohio friends, and when I caught glimpses of their faces during the procession, it was as if my entire youth was passing before my eyes. Former lovers, including Mark, were present, peers with whom I had spent years in high school and college, seminarians from Cambridge, musicians from Boston (the music was exquisite, not pompous or bombastic as if for a coronation), professors, teachers and advisors, persons with whom I have counseled, relatives, aging friends of the family. I also recognized a very special face at the communion rail as I administered the wine chalice — it was the face of Louis, the Puerto Rican migrant worker with whom I had made love eleven years ago in my hometown parish.

After the service, at the outdoor reception in the cathedral garden, a clown appeared in the midst of the crowd and presented me with a bouquet of immense, brightly colored helium-filled balloons. The card read, 'Congratulations and love from your new friends at Emmanuel Church, Southern Pines.' A gay friend turned to me and said, "Zal, they have your number!"

I returned to Southern Pines the next day, when I received your wonderful phone call. I'm embarrassed to write that I cried throughout the ceremony, and when I could control my tears, I would think about you and again I would cry. You were constantly on my mind throughout the day. I wanted you at my side, I wanted you, not me, to kneel before the bishop for the laying on of hands. You must leave Greece, Stephen. You have suffered in exile enough. You can't find a decent job, your attempts at relationships have failed. Please come back to the States. I need you in North Carolina, the Church needs you. You could assist me in my ministry here, or there is an excellent private school nearby where you can teach, or you can do nothing but write, and I will support you, because I love you so much and want you near me. God is clearly calling you to be a priest of the Church, and I am sure I can persuade the Bishop of North Carolina or the Bishop of Ohio to ordain you.

Forgive me, Stephen. Forgive me for losing control, for writing so self-indulgently. But I miss you, and frankly, I'm afraid to face the South without you. I know you well enough to realize that you would never agree to receive the sacrament of ordination unless you could be ordained by your own merits, which include your insistence on candor and self-affirmation as a gay man, your refusal to keep your sexual orientation a secret to anyone — bishops, priests or laity. Because of your integrity, your refusal to bow to pressure from Church officials, you are much more a priest than I shall ever be.

A priest from a depressed steel mill town in Ohio approached me at the ordination reception and said, "So, you're the deacon who is working in Southern Pines, where all the rich people live." I explained to him that although I had lived in Southern Pines only one month, I could assure him that while the Sandhills did indeed consist of a large affluent population, I had also encountered cases of extreme poverty on the outskirts of the resort community. Another person overhearing our conversation observed, "You know, Zal, it must be very difficult to minister to the rich." But I replied that no, it was not all that difficult. When we minister to the rich, we seek primarily to empower them to serve the poor.

Emmanuel Church is a good and warm place, filled with people (almost 700 worship here each Sunday) who are eager to be involved in the life and ministry of the parish. The congregation is active and growing, with a good mix of young families and retirees. Many of the parishioners enjoy an extremely high standard of living, as reflected in luxurious estates and numerous country-club

memberships. Everywhere I drive I see well-manicured
lawns, brilliant flower beds, stately pine forests, sparkling
lakes, rolling golf courses, clay tennis courts, hot tubs and
swimming pools. How will it be possible for me to escape
the trappings of privilege and wealth in such a setting?
What frightens me is that part of me feels that I deserve to
live comfortably, to wear nice clothes, drive a new car,
eat fine food, even belong to a tennis and swimming club
that discriminates against Jewish and black persons. So
deep is my neediness for security, for a sense of style and
self-esteem, that I find myself beginning to strive after
such status symbols. I keep hoping my education, my
position as an ordained minister, and my material gains
will make up for my past feelings of inferiority and powerlessness as a gay person.

My work consists of developing strong music, youth
and outreach programs. In addition to hospital and
nursing home rounds, I'm visiting three families a week,
and if I'm lucky, they invite me for dinner. I love getting
to know parishioners in the setting of their homes or at
their workplace. Some of the dinners, however, can be
tiresome. If I feel bored or unalive at such dinners, must I
feign excitement? If I feel lonely, even though I may be in
the midst of a crowd, must I pretend social interest? When
I meet with my parishioners, I find myself constantly
checking to determine if what I'm saying is consistent
with what I am feeling and who I am.

I have begun a ministry for single persons. There are
plenty of divorced and widowed persons, a smaller group
of unmarried adults, and three lesbians and two gay men
who have come out to me. The majority of singles who
attend our social events come from other churches, or do
not attend any church. Such 'unchurched' singles express

a desire, a need to belong to some social group that does not cater to married heterosexual couples and nuclear families. I have recruited a group of adult parishioners, both single and married, to assist me in leading parish youth programs. The parish is teeming with teenagers who impress me with their earnest passions, the urgency of their relationships, their capacity for love and outrage.

Sam Walker, the rector, has given me the freedom to plan music and liturgy for both the 9 a.m. children's service (and that's what it is — very upbeat and saccharine, and irrelevant to the Gospel message, but popular nonetheless) and the traditional 11 a.m. service. Emmanuel also has a 7:45 a.m. Sunday service which attracts retirees and folks with early tee-off times. I am expected to preach once a month at all three services. I meet with Sam twice a week — once for a staff meeting and once for a supervisory session. He is an excellent teacher, a skilled pastor, a conservative preacher, and a man who is deeply committed to prayer and worship. He also happens to be extremely handsome, but he's more your type than mine. Best of all, he sings beautifully! Sam has taught me that I no longer have to apologize for my combined vocation as a priest and musician. During my education I had often been urged to make a choice between being a priest and a church musician. But these two calls presented themselves to me very early in life as inextricably joined. Emmanuel is a place where I can share my background in sacred music, train as a deacon and later as a priest.

I'm finding that many of these wealthy Southerners are looking for that elusive 'something more' in terms of their relationship with God. One of the great values of a theological education is its enhancement of perspective, enabling me to teach the same truth in different ways instead of knowing only one way of approaching a Christian view of life. As a priest, I want to be able to help individuals from a variety of backgrounds of experience to reflect in their own terms upon their lives as lived in the presence of God. If I can translate or help them translate their faith, their God, into a tangible sense of their lives, or help point the way, strike a chord, touch a heart or mind, then surely I will have done a lot as a curate.

I am keenly aware that individuals rarely express what really matters — the tender, shy, reluctant feelings, the sensitive, fragile, intense feelings. Too often we receive words from people but not the concrete, actual messages and meanings. People will talk on the phone to me for an hour, but they rarely say what they mean. People listen, but there is rarely any real connection or contact with the other. When I am with such persons, I experience deep feelings of loneliness, and I want to break through the empty words and come into touch with the feelings.

Although I have experienced the grace of God in many ways, the one I witness to with greatest conviction from the depths of my own experience is the transformation of feelings; of fear into trust, anger into understanding, loneliness into relatedness, lethargy into hope, grief into acceptance, emotional deadness into love, solemnity into joy, tears into laughter, loss into newness of life. I believe the repression, rejection and denigration of human feelings result in violence, warfare, mental, emotional and physical illness, in quiet desperation and determined protest, in the frantic quest for instant intimacy and cheap, ultimately false short-cuts to self-knowledge.

Part of my vocation as a deacon is to find the person

underneath the mask, to reach for this unique potential, to tap feelings of human compassion. I am thinking here of the loneliness and pain and anguish in associating with people who are playing roles, roles which prevent them from discovering feelings of intimacy, communion and love. Their lives are often filled with too many words, pictures, social engagements and sounds.

Clearly, I must build upon my Christian faith amid the sounds of tearing down, amid the upheavals of anger, neurosis, illness and materialism. As a pastor, I am not a caretaker, a shepherd who with paternalistic concern takes care of weaker creatures. I am not called to interact with human beings as if they are weaker than I. I do not pretend that I can solve other people's problems by quoting a particular Bible verse, but rather, I am willing to accompany them as they struggle to create meaning from their lives, to make themselves vulnerable to loss, change and growth, and to be known as they really are.

With my love,
Zal

❧

Southern Pines, NC
September 16, 1984

Dear Stephen,

Your month on the islands sounded idyllic. Thank you for sending me some of your beautiful photographs. The azure sea and deserted beaches do much to whet my appetite. Next summer I shall join you! You wrote that your travels were conducive to your novel writing. Please send me a chapter or two, as I would love to read it.

I 'came out' as a gay man to Sam this week during our
supervisory session. He didn't seem at all surprised. Either
he had guessed that I was gay, or someone from
Cambridge may have told him of my involvement in gay
rights. I told him about Mark, and confessed that I miss
not having a lover in Southern Pines, but that for the time
being, my parish work is keeping me busy and I am
deriving great satisfaction from friendships with parishioners, a few of whom are aware that I am gay. I was
afraid he would hear about my homosexuality from
another parishioner (perhaps he already has), and wanted
to have the chance to tell him myself. Like many clergy
in the Church today, Sam is struggling to achieve a more
informed and complete knowledge of homosexuality and
its relation to Christianity. He was relieved to learn I was
in therapy, as he admitted that he would have difficulty
discussing gay issues with me.

In fact, we hardly ever touch on any issues at all, let
alone homosexuality. Granted, there is much to keep us
busy at Emmanuel — services, vistitation, pastoral
counseling, youth work, choir rehearsals, Christian
education, Bible study — yet we do little to assist our
parishioners in applying the living Word of God to issues
affecting their personal lives, Church and society. Sam
tends to preach only agreeable sermons. He realizes that
most of the parishioners are traditional Republicans
(indeed, there are many generous contributors to both the
Reagan and Jesse Helms' campaigns), and his view is that
we clergy should refrain from saying or doing anything
which may imprudently antagonize them. Sam always
seems so eager to please everyone, too eager, if you ask
me. I'm especially skeptical when I observe Sam acting
like an obsequious little boy whenever he communicates

with the Bishop of North Carolina, Robert Estill. Sam has
the potential of being a good, strong, charismatic (in the
best sense of the word) Church leader instead of behaving
like a fainthearted rector who seems to collapse at the
first signs of pressure from Bishop Estill.

When I mount the pulpit, I'm sure Sam prays
fervently that I won't say anything too outrageous, such as
publicly declaring myself a gay priest. My style is fairly
simple. I choose a word or a sentence from one of the
Bible readings, and I preach on it, keeping in mind the
particular mix of parishioners at Emmanuel Church, a
congregation consisting of well-educated, affluent
country-club types, three middle-class black families, a
contingent of divorced, widowed and single persons who
usually sit at the back of the church. In my preaching, I
attempt to recognize, touch and affirm all these
individuals, to bring them into contact with God's living
Word, to encourage them to use their gifts to create a
more humane world. If I neglect to express care, respect
and love for each member of that congregation, then I
have failed in my message.

It is in preaching that I find the most creative and
fulfilling intimacy in my relationship with God and
humanity. Intimacy for me occurs whenever there is
extraordinarily rich communication between people.
Sometimes I am troubled by how much I reveal of the
intensity and totality of my attachment to a particular
Old Testament prophet, or one of Jesus' disciples, fearing
that my parishioners will listen to me in a detached way
and find me both indecent and ridiculous. It is very risky
to be honest and forthright (I never preach beyond ten
minutes) in my preaching, because frequently parishioners
do not respond in love, but may react in horror and fear

and strike out aggressively. I frequently get into jams for being politically incorrect, saying what I believe God wants me to say instead of what people want to hear.

Preaching which does not address itself to political issues, to the evils of exploitation, to the inherent dangers of giving divine validation to cultural values, is not letting God have Her way. A church which claims to be politically neutral and impartial is a contradiction of terms. The Gospel is never impartial. That does not mean that it is to be made serviceable for certain parties to use the adjective 'Christian'. But the Gospel as the medium of God's grace participates in Jesus' way to make human life human; and that means going to those — even if it means crucifixion — who by our cultural, economical and political systems and values are kept in hunger, poverty and anxiety. To those who may still be called the marginal people of society, or the wretched of the earth. Who these people are must be decided in every situation anew.

As a preacher, I am an interpreter, a person who makes connections that other people might be missing. I do not essentially tell people what they don't already know, but attempt to show them the meaning and depth of their own experience. I call upon my parishioners to stop, look and listen — to realize what God is doing in their midst. I don't see myself as a persuasive or inspiring preacher. Most of my homilies end as if they were unfinished. I purposely end abruptly, leaving a blank for the parishioner to fill with a personal experience. When I am finished speaking, the homily is still in a fermenting state with people. I hope they leave the Eucharist with something that gradually begins to work its way into their lives. When I preach, I do not employ techniques for changing people in spite of themselves. I am concerned with deepening and enlarging their experience of the Word of God and how it affects contemporary life. In preaching, I attempt to expose myself as an agent of God, and there is resistance in most clergy I know to show themselves as anything, let alone as agents of God.

You asked me how I am getting along with my parents. One of the reasons I accepted the job at Emmanuel was so that I could spend a period of my life near my parents. In addition to adjusting to retirement, my father, himself a surgeon, underwent surgery last year for a tumor. His health is fine now, and both he and Mom have assisted me in getting settled in Southern Pines. It has been a long time since I have spent any time with them, and my three older sisters live in other parts of the country. I regard my proximity to my parents as an opportunity to heal a lot of pain and brokenness in our relationship. Whenever I visit their house, I go with the intention of showing them a good, tension-free time (just like Sam with the bishop), because I'm hoping that if they have it, then I'll get it, too.

Non-acceptance by my parents is perhaps the most difficult side of my life to deal with. Perhaps I was wiser than I thought, when I was younger and didn't care about what my family thought of my homosexuality. Then why, at age 27, do I suddenly have this need for their approval? All my life I've felt hated by my family because I love men. I kept hoping that if only I would excel in my studies, my swimming, my music and my ministry, my family would consider me acceptable, lovable. For my parents, my homosexuality was a crushing revelation, a fact better left unsaid. They wanted three things for me: (1) a career as a physician; (2) a wife who could give birth

to a grandson who would be named Zalmon Omar
Sherwood IX (heaven forbid!); and (3) my happiness,
which was dependent on (1) and (2).

There is a powerful quote from the French existen-
tialist philosopher Jean-Paul Sartre: "We only become
what we are by the radical and deep-seated refusal of that
which others have made us." For the longest time, my
parents' attitude toward my homosexuality was that
"This, too, will pass," but at age 19, I decided, "No, it will
not pass. I am gay. I'm your gay son. Take me or leave
me." And for eight years they have been gradually leaving
me. I want them back. In all that I have done, even in
terms of my relationships with men, I have sought my
parents' support and approval. Moving from Cambridge to
Southern Pines was probably a subconscious gesture of my
trying to conform to their expectations that I would
eventually come to my senses and settle down as a
normal, respectable all-American priest in the Bible Belt
of the country. Now that I am living near them, I realize
the time when I have sought their approval is long past.
More than anything else, I need my own approval.

Growing up, I have learned to tolerate the differences
among family members. How I wish they would recognize
their own trapped narrowness, prejudice and bigotry.
Some days I feel strangled by my parents' conservatism
and fear. Why are they so terrified of me? They cannot
bear to really know or really love me as I am. They
believe that same-sex relationships are immoral, and that
I must be immoral because I commit immoral acts. I have
tried to explain that the sexual component is not always
the main thing in gay relationships, but rather friendship,
mutual support and self-giving love. When I say things
like that, they simply look at me as if I were insane, and

sometimes they can be very good at making me feel insane.

The older I get, the more I tend to resemble my father, both in appearance and temperament. We both have strong, frequently stubborn convictions. Our tempers have flared easily in the past. I feel vulnerable and hypersensitive to his criticism. As a teenager, I remember how, in a fit of exasperation, of frustration about his inability to 'cure' me, he would grasp me by the shoulders, shake me and shout, "What has happened to you? Why are you so different? How could you do such a thing to disgrace our family?" He continues to ask me the same questions. My therapist recommends that I steer clear of my family for my own health and well-being, but despite their homophobia, I love my parents.

I am trying to let go of my frustrated sense of how love should be when I am with my family. There is no "should". There's only an "is", and somehow I've got to accept it, the same way my parents need someday to accept me. There's no doubt at all that they love me very much, but their ability to communicate that love is retarded. Does a steak dinner and a new tennis racket say "we love you"? In their hearts, yes, it does. They raised me, educated me and have expressed their love for me on many occasions. I'm grateful for all they have done to make it possible for me to learn and grow, but it was you, Stephen, and other gay and lesbian friends, who taught me how to love without guilt and fear.

I have a very difficult time fastening my clerical collar each morning and understanding the faith I profess, if that faith gives me no room for understanding, forgiveness and reconciliation when I believe I have been wronged by homophobic colleagues, friends and family members. While my father and I share opposite sides of many issues — many hard, difficult and personal issues — we are both unbelievably intolerant and unforgiving of each other.

I realize we live in an imperfect world and I profess an imperfect faith. But acceptance, understanding, forgiveness and compassion are fairly major elements, and they flow two ways; not only from hurt, close-minded, strong-willed parents who God Knows Why don't have the capacity right now to learn or to accept a God-given reality, my gay identity and sexuality, but also from a son who has experienced harsh judgment, yes, but also infinite love.

I wish we could all walk in each other's shoes. I don't believe there is a clear right and wrong when people who love each other and build their lives on that love hurt so much. But I do believe God's love is powerful enough to heal even that pain, and it is my prayer for my parents and me that it will. In time.

Nothing can ease the pain of losing a family, but I do realize that I am surrounded by other people who love me, who care for me and about me. Some of my parishioners and youth group members seem always to be embracing me in friendship. I love to be touched, to be reminded that I am alive, that someone cares for me, and that I care for others. I've noticed that there are many parishioners who still continue to balk when it comes to passing the Peace during the Eucharist. Some of them embrace the one nearest them in a pew, others offer a handshake, a polite kiss, perhaps just a smile. For some parishioners, that passing of the Peace may be the only gesture of affection they receive all week. It is painful to be human and alone. We need to be touched, and we need to reach out and touch others.

The loneliness of a broken life, a life shattered by betrayal, deceit, rejection, gross misunderstanding, pain, separation. All these severely alter not only my sense of self, but the world in which I live, my relationships and ministry. Despite the relative affluence and isolation of this community, I am struck by how many crises, tragedies, illness and death, poverty and misfortune occur in the daily life of the parish. All I can do as a minister is attempt to create a truly human, full life everywhere. I want to help people laugh and cry, to create joy and lament cruelty, to plunge fully into the moment, to savor all of God's creation. Yet I am aware of how long it has taken me to finally make it, to fully encounter life, to accept the ambiguity, complexity, confusion and pain that arise from being alive.

I am increasingly aware of how complex and demanding every deep relationship is, how much real pain, anger and despair are concealed by most people. I want my music, my ministry, to be life-enhancing, reconciling, liberating and empowering. I search constantly for a balance between the need for prayer and solitude, and the need to be available to my parishioners. I try to remain available, to lose myself in admiration and joy of the other in order to discover the essence of a person. Only then am I aware of the toughness required to survive such intensity of caring and such openness.

Michael's wedding this past week was beautiful. He seems so happy with Kimberly, who is delightful. If anyone has the stamina to be his wife, it's her. Bruce and

Richard came down from Boston for the wedding. They asked all about you, and I gave them your address.

With my love,
Zal

✍

Southern Pines, NC
October 11, 1984

Dear Stephen,

I've been trying to reach you by telephone for days, and this morning I received your short note announcing that you've moved in with Minos. But Stephen, you just met the man! Are you sure you're doing the right thing? I mean, you have always accused me of moving too fast, and here, after less than a week of knowing Minos, you have moved into his Athens apartment. What is so special about this Greek architect, that he is able to win you over so quickly, you who have written repeatedly to me this past year how committed you are to your teaching and writing, and that you have given up on men? Then suddenly, Minos appears in your life! If I sound the least bit concerned, please know that I am also very happy for you. But how I wish I could meet Minos, check him out, talk to him to make sure that he will be a good lover to my best friend. Your description of him is too good to be true. Please send me a photograph of him, and have him take one of you, too. Thanks for your new address, but in your next letter, please include your phone number.

How I envy you being in a relationship! Mark was here for five days at the end of last month, just before he

left for Vienna. We had such a wonderful reunion that I
was tempted to resign my job and follow him to Europe.
He loved Southern Pines and the parish. We played a lot
of tennis (I've become a decent player since I took a few
lessons — more on this later), and one afternoon we
played golf (I'm terrible, but Mark loves the game) with
(are you sitting down?) my parents. I suppose they
approve of Mark because like my father, he is a physician.
Mom and Dad cooked a great meal for us that evening,
and took us for a moonlight cruise in their boat around
the lake. I'm deeply moved when I consider how hard they
tried, and how successful they were, in accepting Mark. If
my parents can accept him, then why can't I?

Mark attended church on Sunday and heard me
preach on Isaiah 5:1 — "Let me sing for my beloved a love
song concerning his vineyard. My beloved had a vineyard
on a very fertile hill." Drawing on my experience of
growing up on a vineyard in Ohio, I preached on God's
celebration of fertility, sensuality and humility both in
nature and in our flesh. That afternoon, Mark accompanied me on my hospital rounds, but he lost his nerve
when it came to attending a youth group meeting, even
though the teenagers would have enjoyed meeting him. I
did have a small dinner party (Mark did most of the
cooking) for six of my single friends (two of whom are
gay), who think I am crazy for separating from him.

Some days I do, too. I do miss Mark, but I still
believe it's important that I continue training as a priest
in this place, without the demands of a full-time relationship. I feel blessed to have made some gay friends here,
but all of them are closeted and harbor so much guilt
about being gay. And you should hear them whine! Why

Southern men feel compelled to whine so much I shall
never understand. Then again, if oppression pervaded
every aspect of my life, and if I didn't know how to cope
with it, then I, too, would start whining.

I am in the midst of my first Southern love affair with
a tennis pro named Justin who teaches at one of the better
clubs. Several weeks ago, after I lost a match to a parishioner, the parishioner sent me a gift certificate for three
private lessons with Justin. He is so gorgeous (age 33, 5'
10", curly brown hair and green eyes which remind me of
you) that the evening I arrived for my first lesson, I could
barely tell him my name let alone swing a racket. He
didn't have much difficulty talking me into taking three
additional lessons, and my game really has improved, as
well as my love life. He asked me to join him for dinner
after our third lesson, and by the fifth lesson, we had
made love at his condominium.

Justin watched Mark and me play tennis one
afternoon. Mark beat me, but I had the pleasure of
introducing him to "my Pinehurst lover." Mark was not
amused. Not only is he jealous, he accuses me of using
Justin, "like you've used every other man you've ever
fucked." I am not using Justin. There is no coercion
involved. When I am making love with Justin, I
experience tenderness, joy, respect, compassion and grace,
all gifts from God who empowers me to share such gifts
with my parishioners. Indeed, it is my sexuality that
provides me with the energy required for ministry, for
communication and life.

This past week was our annual fall diocesan clergy
retreat in Greensboro, North Carolina. I was surprised to
meet seven other gay priests in this diocese, and those

priests tell me there are a lot more gay clergy in North Carolina. All these gay priests (even the ones who came out to me) seem overly concerned with maintaining a self-image of heterosexuality. Most of the gay clergy are married. One gay priest, a cardinal rector of a large Raleigh parish, sent shivers down my spine when he said matter-of-factly, "Don't worry, probably before next fall, you will be married, too." In addition to social acceptance, domestic reasons and family pressure, these priests believe marriage provides social advancement in the Church.

One evening during the three-day retreat, I met in a suite of rooms with a group of young clergy from the diocese. The scene reminded me of something akin to a fraternity house — a group of young men sitting around, drinking beer, cracking dirty jokes and laughing raucously. I had a difficult time understanding much of their Southern humor, but I attribute that to feeling somewhat tired after a day of meeting so many priests. In fact, I was only half-listening when the conversation turned to the topic of homosexuality. I missed hearing some sarcastic remarks about some priest suspected of being gay, but I was fully alert in time to hear a priest tell a gay AIDS joke, after which I announced that I was gay and have friends who are dying from AIDS, and that I objected to vicious gossip and hurtful jokes pertaining to homosexuality.

After several moments of stunned silence, the priest who told the joke apologized to me, and the group began discussing professional football ratings. After a while, I excused myself and began walking outdoors. Another priest, a young rector of a prominent parish in the central part of the diocese, joined me. He invited me to his room for a chat, confessed his homosexuality to me (this man is married to a Southern beauty queen and has three young children), and proceeded to make a pass at me. You know me well enough to know that I would never stoop so low as to sleep with a married man, let alone a priest. He was incredibly persistent in his sexual advances, and when I became angry (and even a bit frightened) and began to leave, he retaliated by stating that I would never get very far professionally as a gay priest in this diocese, and that I had better "face reality" and stay in the closet like all the other gay priests.

There appears to be some tacit agreement among gay clergy to remain closeted, to screw their brother priests during these seasonal retreats, to engage in furtive, anonymous sex in bookstores or restrooms in cities near their parishes. Many diocesan clergy have expressed hostility toward me, not only because I refuse to sleep with them, but because I am at ease with my homosexuality and appear to be popular with my parishioners. Indeed, it is remarkable how many parishioners have been able to accept my gayness, given the homophobic clergy's reluctance to discuss any issues of human sexuality. The argument many priests give against educational programs about homosexuality is that the laity cannot handle such a controversial subject. Nonsense! I've been at Emmanuel long enough to know that both my teenage and adult parishioners are quite capable of grappling with this issue. It's the closeted gay clergy and bishops who suppress such educational programs, because they realize the more people learn about homosexuality, the greater likelihood that these same priests and bishops will be exposed in all their arrogance, self-righteousness, dishonesty and hypocrisy.

I'm glad your teaching is going so well this year. Remember how we seminarians used to dread youth work, how we considered it nothing more than glorified babysitting? And yet there you are, teaching English at a Greek secondary school while I travel with forty teenagers and four adult advisors to Myrtle Beach for a weekend retreat. I actually look forward to parish youth meetings and events. I am blessed with a group of adult advisors who assist me in planning programs and are committed to providing youths with the space and freedom to explore issues of faith, relationships, decision-making and responsibility. Since we welcome and encourage youths from different denominations and faiths to participate, we do not insist that everyone join in Bible study or worship activities. We spend a lot of time discussing our varieties of religious experience, but our main purpose is to share in friendship, recreation, community building and outreach.

The youth group has a strong sense of justice, love and respect for all people. It hurts them to see anyone viewed or treated unjustly. Upon discovering an injustice, they will demand in disbelief, "Why isn't anyone doing anything about that?" and, after some thought and prayer, they proceed to take action to serve people in need. They have learned, at such an early age, to care about God, to care about something or someone, to accept their responsibility for the welfare of every other living being. They question the relevance and purpose of any program the advisors and I introduce. I admire their constant critical gaze, their directness and spontaneity, their aversion for religious sham of any sort, their insistence that we be

authentic in all that we do, in all that we believe, in the
ways we love.

With my love,
Zal

✌

Southern Pines, NC
November 26, 1984

Dear Stephen,
　　I've just finished reading, for the third time, the first
part of your novel, and per your request, I'm sending you
several pages of my thoughts on your work. I'm naturally
a biased reader, since I have always loved everything you
have written, and this novel is especially beautiful. Thank
you for sharing it with me, and when you are ready,
please send me more. From talking with you, however, it
seems that Minos has been interfering with your writing
schedule. You must keep at it, Stephen. Your fiction,
much more than any homily I could preach, has the
potential of leading people to the truth about themselves.
Even though you don't specifically mention any Christian
theme, your novel breathes the atmosphere of the
Christian moral and cosmic world-view. Your fiction, in
its depiction of the human condition as one of need and
alienation, may aid the unbeliever to come to the Gospel.
I've always believed literature and the arts vividly embody
the major doctrines of Christian faith in a form of
expression that people can assimilate much more readily
than they can the conceptual forms which most
theologians offer. Your writing symbolizes what the
Realm of God might be, what our yearning awaits.
　　My church work has been animated by the idea that

the parish's worship and outreach activities can only be enhanced by the presence of artistic creativity. I have always been interested in the influence of musical and visual forms on the political and religious climate of all historical periods. When we talk about artists and musicians, we are talking about people whose chief pursuit is in a field of disclosure which uses non-verbal symbols to express rational ideas. Theologians are shy of musicians and artists for this very reason. Whatever expresses ideas without words is suspect in the sight of those who serve the Word. This suspicion should be easy to allay; for the Word is not and never was merely words, but is flesh.

I believe that the Church needs to take even more seriously the vocation of artists in our midst, and that it is the responsibility of the Church to empower women and men to make an imaginative use of their own experience in worship, in outreach and in their own lives. One of my favorite tasks as an ordained minister is to build communities, groups of people, whether choir members, youth group members or single adults. If I have any function, it is to help the Church receive gifts of all its members, so that the Church might be a source of hope and healing for society. My creative role is to set people free, to tap their talents, to make life and ministry accessible to all of them regardless of age, race, sex and social status. I am called to share with others what I have only imperfectly received for myself, a sense of vocation and the experience of living in the power of love which is Christ.

Sometimes I feel that I am not free to respond creatively to the awesome demands of history and the joyful ones of the Holy Spirit. I must learn, without fear or guilt, to think and act creatively. It is an element of balance that is lacking in my life. A 'mixed life,' both active and contemplative, is difficult for me to sustain. It is difficult because my parishioners are so demanding. I seem overly concerned that I accomplish a set number of things, that I make some tangible contribution to the parish community, that I 'do' something that shows that my presence makes a difference. In trying to keep busy and setting before myself a variety of tasks to perform, I so often overlook the greatest gift which God gives to ministers, both lay and ordained, which is our ability to enter into solidarity with those who suffer, and not only with those who suffer, but also with those who rejoice.

I love solitude. Every minister and musician has to, because without it there is no opportunity for serious study and rehearsal. Yet there is a sense of alienation from humanity that increases when, year after year, one is forced to think that people are a distraction from one's real work. I used to think that alienation was to be expected, because in seminary, priests would constantly remind us that a priestly vocation involves a detachment from Western society's bonds of excessive affluence, violence, hatred and manipulation. Yet how can we ever critique and change unjust social conditions unless we fully expose ourselves to the ways of the world? I am haunted by the thought that I have not lived, I have not entered, I have not allowed myself to be loved, to be caught up in the events surrounding me. There comes a time when I can no longer keep at arm's length from life, when I must wager and risk, when I must truly experience and understand persons and events with the greatest of intensity. After all, the Church is not validated on its social, cultural or aesthetic merits, but because the Word was made flesh, and we are all members of the body of Christ.

I'm counseling three gay parishioners — two married men and a married woman. All are in their late thirties. The woman is married to a doctor, and is the mother of four children, two of whom are in my youth group. She met her lover at the university where she is working on her master's degree, and plans to move in with her after the holidays. I wish she would move now, as her husband and kids, not to mention people in town, are making life miserable for her. The woman is a beautiful, rich socialite, but when she came to my office this morning, she had a black eye and broken tooth from fighting with her husband last night. Ironically, her divorce lawyer is one of the gay married men I am counseling. The other man is a salesman. Even though both men have lovers, they are a long way from leaving their wives and children. Their wives are aware of their homosexual affairs, and seem to condone them as long as their husbands continue to pay the bills and maintain a heterosexual image in public.

During a supervisory session with Sam, he asked me the names of the gay parishioners I am counseling, but of course I could not tell him, even after he demanded them, because I would have breached confidentiality. He said he needed to know, "for the good of the parish. Something like this could be explosive," and proceeded to surmise that these particular parishioners were "probably not gay, but just suffering from some mid-life crisis." He is of the view that if you're married, and you discover you have homosexual feelings, you should repress them. I'm tired of hearing all these religious leaders telling us that self-denial is the way of the Cross. For me, self-denial is my willingness to accept and love myself as I really am, a gay man, with all my human imperfections, but without any elements of self-pretension and self-illusion. Denying my false self enables me to reveal my true self, and brings me to a deeper awareness of the real situation in my life and the lives of my parishioners.

Justin and I attended a wonderful dinner party last weekend at the mansion of one of my gay parishioners, a successful horse trainer. It was a large gathering of gay men — other horse trainers, stablehands, golf and tennis pros. I sat next to the handsome lover of one of the trainers, and was surprised to learn that he works as a male stripper. I had never met one before, have you? His name is Ted, and he is a fascinating person, one of the best conversationalists I have met in the South. We plan to spend more time together in what he refers to as 'Suffering' Pines. By the way, he was not at all surprised to learn that I was an Episcopal minister, and proceeded to entertain me with hilarious stories about his closeted, ordained patrons. I wish you could have been there, as after dinner, the host began playing a compact disc, and one by one, guests began to rise and dance. I haven't danced so much since you left Boston. They all were such talented dancers (especially the stripper), so free and at ease with their bodies, as if celebrating a liturgical dance of the soul.

For my birthday, Justin gave me a lovely bowl thrown by a local potter. It has the most intricate blue glaze. Both the choir and youth group had parties for me within the octave of my birthday. The youth group provided Thanksgiving Day dinners for four Moore County poor families. We roasted turkeys at the church since none of the families had working ovens. The youths were so concerned that all the families received enough food to last them through Christmas, when we will bring more food and gifts to the same families. Taking food to these families was a profound experience for many of the teenagers. They met people who know hunger well enough to live every day fearing it. We witnessed the struggle, the gnawing desperation of a poor white mother and her two shoeless children (we brought them shoes the next day), a black family of nine living in a cold, three-room shanty, an elderly woman and her wheelchair-bound, emotionally-disturbed daughter, and a Cambodian refugee family of five. All these people somehow managed to express thanks this past holiday, even though they must fight daily for their human dignity in the face of odds much greater than those I shall ever know as a gay man.

I've learned that my Ohio bishop, James Moodey, will not be ordaining me to the priesthood. Normally, I would be ordained to the priesthood this winter, but in North Carolina, Bishop Estill requires deacons to serve for an entire year before ordination. Since I want to remain in this diocese for at least three more years, I will postpone my ordination until June. I'd much prefer that Bishop Moodey ordain me, since he is aware of my homosexuality, but he will not be able to travel to Southern Pines in June. I have been praying for a tactful, timely and pastoral method (is there such a thing?) to come out as a gay man to Bishop Estill. My friends and colleagues say that it will mean sudden death in terms of my ordination to the priesthood. Perhaps I should just continue to perform the tasks before me and let my record speak for itself. Coming out seems so pointless, so selfish and irresponsible to most Southerners, but God will not allow me to remain silent when there are so many people who are struggling to discover their sexual identities, so many people searching for ways to love, and so few publicly observable gay role models from which to choose in the South. Because I have been more and more open with parishioners about my homosexuality, it has taken additional energy for me to contend with rejection, criticism and hostility of people who are offended by my candor and gay lifestyle. I have discovered, however, that it takes even more energy to please people by doing what they want me to do, to conform to heterosexist norms and attitudes.

Just the other day, one of the most prim and proper Southern belle parishioners asked if I would consider escorting her visiting sister to the holiday benefit dance for the hospital. When I explained that I was gay and did not date women, she immediately stopped smiling, drew back in disbelief, and for a while, I thought the pretty young woman before me was going to faint. After a spell, she composed herself with the best of manners, resumed her radiant smile, and drawled, "That's all right, Zal, I still love you, even if you are gay." She kept looking back at me with a concerned look in her eyes as she made her way to the door of my office, and before leaving, she said, "Do let me know, Zal, if you decide to change your mind. I'm sure my sister would enjoy your company. We needn't tell her a thing."

Your and Minos' Christmas presents are on their way. How I wish we could celebrate the holidays together.

With my love,
Zal

❧

Southern Pines, NC
January 15, 1985

Dear Stephen,

It seems like ages since I talked with you on Christmas Eve. Thank you for calling, and thank you and Minos for the beautiful print. I think you would approve of the frame I selected. When my friends stop by to admire the print, it pleases me to tell them that it came from you.

Christmas was a season of prayerful anticipation, sharing, festive music, holly and pine, joy and celebration. So many parishioners had holiday parties, and I felt obligated to make an appearance at each of them. Christmas Day was sunny and warm enough for tennis, but as I reported on the phone, Justin and I are no longer partners.

As Ted (my friend, the stripper) pointed out, "Lovers come and go, but friends last forever." Justin and I stopped seeing each other shortly before Christmas. I had so little time for him during December, and I think he became tired of playing second fiddle to the Church. He's currently running a tennis clinic at a club in Palm Beach, where I had planned to vacation following the holidays. Instead, I spent five days in wintry New York visiting friends, shopping for books and music, catching a few recitals and a play.

The first night I arrived in New York, I dined with a priest and his lover, and almost immediately they began naming all their friends who have been diagnosed with AIDS. After hearing their list, I had no appetite. The next day I visited a musician friend whom I hadn't seen in years. I could barely recognize his emaciated, hairless body in the hosptial room. He was glad to see me, and had heard that I had been ordained.

"How," he asked me, "could you become so involved in an institution that oppresses gay persons, rips our families apart, pressures our lovers to abandon us, encourages our bosses to fire us, leaves our landlords no choice but to evict us from our apartments, so thoroughly and completely assaults our sense of dignity and worth, shatters our whole lives?" I made some insipid remark such as, "I hope I can be an instrument for reform and change in the Church," but after a mere seven months on the job, I realize I will never be able to affect the majority of Episcopalians' attitudes toward gay persons. My friend lay dying because he had loved too much, and I am, by virtue of my ordination, my silence, my reluctance to speak out against this insidious disease, responsible for his illness.

Too many Church leaders have continued to condemn our right to make love and to form stable relationships. Gay men and lesbians are actively discouraged from developing sustained relationships, because such relationships threaten to blow the cover of gay priests who choose to remain closeted. For fear of arousing speculation about themselves, priests avoid socializing with gay and lesbian couples in their parishes. When asked to perform blessings of homosexual unions, these same priests use the lame excuse that their bishop won't allow such services, and that the priest's livelihood would be threatened if word spread that he or she approved of such unions.

In the Church's failure to celebrate and bless our relationships, our sexuality, many of us have felt forced to hide our gayness, to seek anonymous sex with strangers, to look for love in all the wrong places, where we run a

higher risk of being infected with the AIDS virus. As a
result, our friends are dying. If only AIDS would lead us
gay people to rebel against this sort of oppression and to
become visibly committed to our gay identities.

The interpretation of AIDS as God's judgment on
homosexuality infuriates me, but many of my Southern
gay friends tend to take such a charge seriously, resulting
in their feeling more guilty, powerless and undeserving of
love. We have been blamed for our own suffering as the
Falwells and Schlafleys of the world continue to try to lay
on us gay persons the responsibility for the very existence
of AIDS. The popularity achieved by simplistic, fundamentalist religions is a sign of unthinking reaction to the
tragedy. This kind of religion allows people to ignore
other people's reality. It encourages people to turn their
backs, in some cases to cheer, while human beings suffer
and die.

Still, despite all their ranting and raving, these
fundamentalist Christians have something to teach us
regarding issues of choice and responsibility, words which
many of us gay persons shy away from. Should we gay
men not face the fact that the promiscuous nature of the
stereotypically gay lifestyle is, in part, to blame for the
outbreak of AIDS? Is it not true that if we did not choose
to fuck each other, we wouldn't be faced with this threat?
Can we accept the responsibility for the risks involved in
choosing to have sex with other men without supporting
the disabling belief that AIDS is a natural consequence of
our lifestyle or punishment dished out by an indignant
God?

The attacks from the reactionary right hold the
potential for making us more defensive and pushing us
further into the murky quicksand of living as victims by

enticing us to deny once more any responsibility for our sexuality. For too long gay men have used the rhetoric of victimization in an effort to gain sympathy from those who might otherwise condemn us. I am tired of hearing gay men whine to their critics, "If we could choose, of course we wouldn't choose to be gay. We can't help it if God created us this way."

If only we were able to say instead, "While I cannot take credit for my homosexual feelings, I do choose to be gay and I affirm the goodness of my sexuality," perhaps we would be in a better position to accept responsibility for our actions. We do have a choice about how we live and relate to other human beings. We will be much better off when we are able to take credit for our choice to reject heterosexist values and assumptions that male/female genital relationships are innately superior to same-sex relationships.

After all, we could have chosen to deny or repress our desires to relate sexually with members of our own sex. We could have struggled to live by the rules of the established, heterosexual order. We could have chosen to remain celibate. But at some point in his life every sexually active gay man has chosen to act on his feelings. In doing so, each of us has made a sociological, political and ethical statement. Going against the norms and taboos of a society is to rebel against the system. It is a form of civil disobedience. In North Carolina, homosexual acts are legally defined as 'crimes against nature.' I will not be labeled a pervert, a sinner or a criminal. I will not be defined out of the institutional Church for choosing to make love to another man.

We are being warned repeatedly of the risks involved in having sex with multiple partners and of participating in certain forms of sexual activity which appear to increase the risk of contracting the dread disease. No sexually active gay man can afford to simply shrug his shoulders and ignore the risks involved in uncaring, indiscriminate sexual activity. We have stopped tricking with strangers, stopped patronizing baths and backroom bars, resorted to using condoms or have chosen to avoid participating in those activities which have been implicated in AIDS. Still others have begun to speak more favorably of monogamous relationships or have chosen to confine their sexual involvements to a select circle of friends. A few have resorted to celibacy, afraid to touch, afraid to risk, afraid to make love, just fighting to stay alive.

I have visited three AIDS patients at our local hospital. I would never have learned about them had I not been friends with one of the hospital nurses, who notified me when they were admitted. Trying to be of help to the healing and growth of these AIDS patients has been like putting an image of myself on a razor blade again and again. I am never sure of what or whom I will encounter when I walk into their isolated hospital rooms. Often the content of my hospital visits appears to be more on a bridge-party level, but even those conversations help to pass the patients' long days. Some afternoons, I simply sit with these AIDS patients and watch soap operas while we lust for a particular actor. Often my patients and I speak about our feelings and our relationships. We share meaningful silences and emotional tears. I feel a need to pray with all my patients, but if they object to praying out loud, I pray silently in their presence. Many times I take the initiative to help give form and words to patients' crises of faith. I learn every day to deal with their hope and fear, denial and loneliness, love and anguish. My encounters with patients in the hospital, much as they are riddled with my blind spots, gropings-about, failures of insight, are integral to my formation as a priest, a healer of souls.

Yet it is not the AIDS patients who require healing. In New York, I participated in an immense healing service, during which hundreds of persons with AIDS came to the front of the church, knelt down and received the laying on of hands for healing from a contingent of ordained ministers. My heart beat wildly and my hands trembled as I began laying my hands on the heads of these young men. Then, as I observed my ordained colleagues in their expensive vestments, I thought, "Something is wrong here," and immediately I left the sanctuary with tears streaming down my face. It is not the AIDS patients who require healing, but the Church and its ordained ministers. Persons with AIDS are more effective channels of God's grace and power than I shall ever be. It is I who should be kneeling before persons with AIDS, it is we ordained clergy who are sick, closeted, repressed, and desperately in need of forgiveness and healing from these individuals who have the courage to reach out and love someone, to suffer and die in order to redeem our lesbian and gay identities as God's lovers in the world.

I preached a children's homily this past Sunday on the baptism of Jesus in the Jordan River, and brought in a live white dove to symbolize the Holy Spirit. Everything was fine until the dove got away from the children and began flying around the sanctuary, only to defecate on the carpet leading up to the communion rail! I'm off next weekend

to the North Carolina mountains for a youth ski retreat.
I'm always concerned that one of the youths might get
hurt on the slopes, but I'm sure they can ski circles
around me.

With my love,
Zal

❧

Southern Pines, NC
March 14, 1985

Dear Stephen,

It's spring in Southern Pines and I'm in love again!
There are so many different kinds of trees, shrubs and
flowers in bloom that the place resembles a fairyland, and
as Ted quips, "You and I are the only fairies in town!"

I met Dennis two weeks ago at the local gym where I
have been working out this winter. He teaches high
school history and coaches the football and track teams.
He had planned a career in professional football, but
during college, he injured his knee. He has many of my
youth group teenagers in class and on his teams. He's the
most closeted man I've ever been with, and I had to pledge
that I would not discuss our affair with anyone. You must
think that I am out of my mind! You realize that I would
never agree to hide my relationship with another man, but
in this instance, I have had to compromise. Dennis is
black, and in the South, people have difficulty accepting
interracial marriages, let alone interracial homosexual
relationships. Dennis could lose his job if our relationship
were discovered. He has met Ted, and doesn't object to
letting him know about us, but beyond that, the affair is a

secret. But Stephen, it's worth it. He is a beautiful man with the most refreshing smile, so concerned about his students, so aware of the events affecting our lives, so enraged about racism and poverty in the South, apartheid in South Africa. As for his lovemaking — Southern gentlemen, despite being so uptight about coming out, are so much more passionate, more tender and caring than any of my Yankee lovers.

One evening last week, I accompanied Dennis to his church, a small, all-black Pentecostal church about ten miles south of Southern Pines. Although I was the only white person present, I was warmly welcomed by the 24-member congregation and the pastor, who was a small, elderly black woman with a booming voice. We sang Gospel hymns, clapped hands, locked arms and swayed to the music. The pastor preached for over a half hour, mesmerizing me with her fierce devotion to the Gospel and its message of salvation to her congregation. Afterwards, she laid her tiny, calloused hands on two sick people and prayed aloud until they rose and praised God for their miraculous healing. My faith is miniscule compared to the faith of the worshipers gathered in that small rural church. Our liturgies at Emmanuel resemble mere play-acting next to the authentic, spontaneous and binding communion of the black church.

We're in the middle of Lent, and while I have not given up men, I have been fasting two days a week. You've probably heard the following adage — "It's not what you give up during Lent that matters, but rather, what you give." Yet how can we truly reach out and give to our sisters and brothers, unless we first undergo a period of prayer and fasting, of self-emptying, of letting go of the

many foods, distractions and habits we depend on, so that
we become truly free, available and present to those who
need us?

Fasting helps me understand hungry people. When I
fast and experience the pain of hunger, I can never forget,
never fail to recognize and respond to the hunger of
others. Dennis tells me that all social movements and
organizations were born of hunger. Not privatized hunger
or hunger kept to oneself, but hunger shared. Poverty
shared. Oppression shared. The evil, bitter taste and
experience of racism, sexism, ageism, militarism — all
shared.

In the Ash Wednesday Gospel, Jesus counsels us not
to look dismal when we are fasting, but if through fasting,
I become in touch with the hunger and pain of others,
how can I possibly not look dismal, not lament loudly,
not cry out against the suffering and injustice before my
eyes? Liberation and healing begin when hunger is
acknowledged and allowed to be pain. From there hunger
becomes shareable, and where possible, resolvable.

I've been spending Thursdays (my day off) in
Durham, where I help other gay men prepare and serve
hot lunches to about sixty poor, mostly black people. It's
very different from the soup kitchen in Boston where you
and I used to volunteer. For some reason, the people who
come for food in Durham do not seem quite as sad and
desperate as those endless lines of cold and hungry people
in Boston. I am always impressed with black Southerners'
strong sense of faith, their vast knowledge of the Bible,
their understanding that God favors the poor and
oppressed over the rich and privileged. And please explain
to me, Stephen, why all these soup kitchens are usually
staffed by volunteers from the lesbian and gay

community? I think many of us gay persons live in terror
that someday, we might be forced to stand in line for food
at a soup kitchen. I have a recurring nightmare that I will
lose my job on account of my homosexuality, that no one
will hire me because I am gay, that I will never settle
down with a lover, that I will grow old, suffer intense
loneliness and die alone in some tenement building.
Romantic illusion? I used to think so, but I keep meeting
elderly lesbians and gay men who fit such a description.

After serving lunches on Thursdays, I spend two
hours practicing the Flentrop organ at the Duke
University chapel. It's a magnificent instrument and the
immense Gothic chapel is an inspiring place for music
making. I've made friends with a Duke undergraduate
lesbian named Charlotte, who happens to be the grand-
daughter of one of my elderly parishioners in Southern
Pines. She is one of the few persons I have met here who
shares an interest in feminist and peace issues. We talk
idealistically of setting up a gay and lesbian household
somewhere, and I have often thought to myself, that if
ever I decide to have children, I would ask Charlotte to be
the mother.

Late Thursday afternoons, I meet with my therapist
in Chapel Hill. He practiced law for many years before
returning to school for a doctorate in clinical psychology.
He has done a lot of legal aid and advocacy work on behalf
of minorities, and has been helpful in strengthening my
pastoral counseling skill with women, adolescents, black
persons and sexual minorities. In other words, he's
teaching me how to be an advocate, and in the process,
has healed much of the pain I experience in the South as a
gay man.

Charlotte and I both attend Integrity meetings which

are held on Thursday night in Durham. Several months ago, Bishop Estill and a priest who directs diocesan social ministries asked Durham-area clergy to form an Integrity chapter to minister to the needs of the gay and lesbian community. While I am impressed by the responses from both clergy and gay persons, I resent Church leaders who view gays as persons 'to be helped.' Rather than patronizing us with support groups like Integrity, the Church needs to find ways of publicly ritualizing and celebrating experiences of lesbians and gay men.

I've been criticized by clergy for not wearing my clerical collar at the meetings, but frankly, I do not attend Integrity meetings in any official capacity, but rather as a gay man seeking friendship with other gay persons. Most Integrity members are aware that I am an ordained deacon, but most importantly, they appreciate the fact that I have come out to them as a gay man, since the other attending clergy (most of whom are also gay) prefer to talk about gays in the abstract, sit on the sidelines, available for ministry, but observing from a safe distance. These same priests have the nerve to proposition me for sex following the meetings, and when I refuse, they walk off in a huff and start flirting with some vulnerable Integrity member.

One of these priests, an Episcopal monk who has taken a vow of chastity, visited Southern Pines two weeks ago for a preaching mission at Emmanuel, and spent the night at my house. After trying unsuccessfully to coax me into his bed, he told me how concerned he and other clergy were about me, that my reputation was on the line, that priests considered me to be indiscreet when it came to flaunting (his word) my homosexuality. He also told me that he and other priests were planning to boycott my

ordination to the priesthood in June, since they, in all
good conscience (again, his words), would somehow feel
tainted (whatever that means) if they were to publicly
express support for my ministry.

"We do not believe," he said, "that you have been
deporting yourself in a manner suitable for that of a priest
of the Church. How then, could you possibly expect us to
participate in your ordination?" I wished him goodnight
and went directly to bed.

How I wish you would have been available to help me
teach a Bible study class on the first chapter of Romans!
Sam usually teaches the weekly Tuesday morning Bible
study class, but just before last week's class, he was called
away on an emergency and asked me to substitute for
him. So there I was, in the company of twenty women
and three retired men (one of whom is a General), and all
of us opened our Bibles to the first chapter of Romans. Let
me refresh your memory of Romans 1:26-27 — "God gave
them up to dishonorable passions. For not only did their
females exchange natural intercourse for that which is
against nature, but also males, leaving natural intercourse
with females, lusted in their desire for one another, males
working shame with males and receiving the punishment
within themselves which their falsehood necessitated."

So what would you have done? I launched a discussion of homosexuality (my knees trembling throughout
the exercise), and was amazed to hear such a wide
diversity of opinions from what I had pre-judged as a
homogenous, conservative group of Bible study partic-
ipants. There were several readers, two charismatics in
particular, who interpreted these verses as a flat-out
condemnation of all homosexual activity. They impressed
me with their ability to quote several other chapters and

verses which appear to condemn gay persons as sleazy, evil anti-God people.

Others, including, most amazingly, the General, disapproved of using the Bible as a weapon for cruelly wounding the gay minority. They pointed out that the biblical texts that are being used to castigate and exclude gay men and lesbians are the same kind of biblical proof texts used by another generation to exclude blacks and women from full participation in the Church. They stressed the importance of examining Scripture in an open and careful way while recognizing that God's acts of justice and mercy are still at work in today's world. These readers were able to distinguish between sexual orientation and immoral sexual activity, and shared stories about their lesbian and gay friends who have lived for years in committed, caring homosexual relationships.

I was praying that our discussion might end on that note, but a dear elderly woman pointed out that gay persons can be denied jobs, denied housing and access to public accommodations, lose custody of their children, and even be arrested if they choose to have sexual relationships with other consenting adults of their own sex. One of the charismatics brought up the issue of the ordination of gay persons, and for a moment, my heart stopped beating. Several elderly parishioners countered by saying that they had known many gay men who had served as exemplary priests. Then, a fashionable young vestry member looked at me and said, "But you know, Zal, if I thought you were gay, I would not be able to support you for ordination to the priesthood. Some things just aren't appropriate for Church leaders."

There was a period of uncomfortable silence, and I suggested we continue discussing other aspects of Paul's

epistle. What a coward I am! This woman gave me the
perfect chance to come out to this special group of lay
leaders, and rather than place my life and ministry in
God's hands, I chose instead to skirt the issue, to run
away and hide beneath the shroud of Paul's convoluted,
theological arguments.

How can this be happening to me, Stephen? Why do I
seem so concerned about what people think, why do I fear
the consequences of revealing this essential part of my
whole self? Is ordination, and the security that goes with
it, so important to me that I would be willing to sell my
soul and become just like the other priests whom I have
been describing in this letter? Most of my parishioners
don't want to hear about, don't want to be confronted
with, the issue of my homosexuality. They seem
interested only in my musical and youth activities, and
would probably not be pleased with my prophetic theories
on para-cultures, even if many of them are in life
situations which are directly relevant to them. There is no
obvious bridge from me to my parishioners. There is,
however, a common bridge in that we love God and are
seeking to do God's will.

With my love,
Zal

ℛ

Southern Pines, NC
April 23, 1985

Dear Stephen,

I'm finally slowing down after a busy Lent and Easter
season. The weather has become pleasantly warm, and
I've been taking time to play a lot of tennis and golf. My

gay friends accuse me of being a country-club priest, but I
try to explain to them that playing such sports is one of
the most effective ways of getting to know my parishioners. After a four-hour afternoon on the golf course, I
manage to learn almost everything there is to know about
the three other members of the foursome. And in between
sets of tennis, my opponents invariably make some
startling confession while we're mopping our brows and
sipping iced water. Some of my most meaningful pastoral
encounters with parishioners have taken place during
cocktail hour in their hot tubs.

I refuse to feel guilty about taking advantage of such
perks, but instead thoroughly enjoy being outdoors with
folks who want very much to be able to relate to me. I
resent well-meaning friends who tell me that as a gay
man, I should be ministering to disenfranchised people in
San Francisco or New York. I am skeptical of people who
try to ghettoize us gay persons, who want to ship us off to
a more tolerant environment where we may be among
others of our own ideology and persuasion.

While I am committed to the concept of urban
ministry, God has placed me in Southern Pines, where I
have the chance to minister to many different kinds of
people. Several affluent parishioners, who seem to have
everything that money can buy, frequently stop by my
office in a state of acute depression. Their marriages are
failing, their children are experimenting with alcohol and
drugs, their lives are haunted by past mistakes and missed
opportunities. It would all seem so banal if it were not for
their intense degree of suffering. I cannot pretend to
understand completely the root of their suffering, but I
offer myself as a companion while together the parish-

ioner and I seek ways to heal those broken parts of our lives. Many of my clergy colleagues insist the only way we can heal ourselves is to stop pitying ourselves and continue to reach out and minister to those who are truly needy, as if some human needs are more important than others. None of us ministers, lay or ordained, can be effective in our ministries unless we first take the time and make the effort to care for ourselves, to seek help from others in meeting some of our needs.

After the last service on Easter Day, I traveled with my youth group to Washington, D.C. Michael met us one afternoon and took us on a tour of the National Cathedral. He was wonderful to our group. He shared some fascinating information about various parts of the cathedral and took time to answer all of the youths' questions. While the teenagers made some brass rubbings in the cathedral gift shop, I had a chance to talk with Michael. He seems very happy and is still very much in love with Kimberly.

During our conversation, Michael told me that two lesbian couples and one gay couple had recently asked him to bless their relationships.

"Did you help them write their ceremonies?" I asked.

"Why, no," he said. "I told them that as a priest of the Episcopal Church, I was not permitted by my bishop to bless their unions."

Can you believe it? Michael wouldn't even agree to bless privately the union of these couples! He said he was afraid that word of such a ceremony might reach the bishop, who would then discipline him.

"I don't understand you, Michael," I said. "I don't understand how you can agree to, for instance, bless the hounds at your father-in-law's ritzy hunt club, but then refuse to bless the relationships among your gay brothers and sisters."

One of my primary functions as a priest is to affirm and bless all God-centered, human relationships without fear of reprisal from my bishop or any other ecclesiastical authority. In withholding his blessing, Michael is failing to affirm and celebrate the gift of God's love in the lives of those gay and lesbian couples. I even went so far as to describe his non-action as sinful, as damaging their dignity, alienating them from the Church, making them feel less worthy of God's grace and blessing. Whenever we say "no" to God's love in its multitudinous forms, we are sinning.

Your birthday present is on its way, along with a book of poems by the early 17th-century priest, George Herbert. I recently had the best time working with a retired English teacher who helped me prepare an hour-long parish adult forum on his poetry, which depicts a person torn by inner conflicts, tensions between love and sin which we all experience. The suffering and passion of Lent and Holy Week, and the glory of Christ's Resurrection at Easter, stirred Herbert's heart and imagination time and again in his poems. Christ is the one who lives, loves, challenges, heals, suffers, dies, rises, redeems and transforms. It is the transforming power of the risen Christ that invests all our lives with possibility, meaning, purpose and love.

Dennis had two days off from school last week, and we drove to the coast. We tried to check in at a beachfront motel, and the woman at the front desk looked suspiciously at Dennis and me and said, "This is a family motel. We don't allow any partyin' to go on in these rooms." I told her that there was no need to worry, as I was an Episcopal priest and Dennis was my lover, and at that point, she almost fainted. Dennis was furious with me as we drove on to a more accommodating motel. We ended up arguing and making love most of the time we were at the beach, and by the time we returned to Southern Pines, we had decided to stop seeing each other. Lately I've been resenting how closeted our relationship is, and frankly, Dennis' homophobia became too much for me to handle, as it constantly seemed to be nibbling away at my self-respect. If it is truly impossible for me to commit myself to a person, how can it be possible for me to commit myself to my ordination vows and the parish?

As the ordination approaches, I find that I need separate space and more time to identify and analyze the various aspects of my life and ministry. I need a chance to build my strength and confidence, and rid myself of self-denigrating attitudes and behavior. One of the best ways to regain my strength is through prayer and meditation. In the busy life of the parish, it has not always been easy for me to maintain a degree of inner tranquility. I now rise an hour earlier and take the phone off the hook in order to spend time praying and meditating on the daily Bible lectionary.

One of the things I have concluded through prayer is that I must come out to Bishop Estill. I've been procrastinating, because there have been days when I felt that God wants me to simply live my life without explanation. If I were to come out to Bishop Estill, it would be as though I was asking permission or seeking approval. If I would live my life without apology or explanation, would I not be making a bolder statement? I don't know the answer to such a question, but repeatedly in my prayer life I have discerned that God wants me to reveal my whole self to the bishop. Everyone pleads with me to wait at least until after the ordination, that such information is not pertinent to my relationship with the bishop, that indeed, the bishop is not entitled to know certain aspects of our private lives. I've started making a list of how often other clergy tell me to wait, to be patient when it comes to my espousing various projects and causes. The word 'wait' smacks of conservatism — political, social and ecclesiastical. I am impatient with the way things are. I throw myself into the nuclear disarmament debate, fight for the rights of women and minorities, insist that our worship services be inclusive and relevant to the world around us.

I have discovered two dimensions of the word 'wait' as I attempt to live out my life. They are held together in tension — an eager longing, a passionate expectancy which sends us out into the world to meet God at work and play; and the willingness to accept the fact that we will never receive everything or everyone on time and by our terms, but rather by God's time and by God's terms.

As a novelist and musician, you and I are aware that in the exercise of art, patience is paramount. In your writing, you brood over a chaos of formless energy — memories, thoughts, feelings, images — and make a pattern of it, reducing it to literary order. Perhaps once or twice in my youth, I have come close to experiencing a form of divine grace that comes from rehearsing my music with discipline and patience. A true artist knows how to wait.

One of my parishioners, a woman in her sixties, visited me today in my office and began talking about her 29-year-old son who, after serving three years as an assistant priest, came out as a gay man to his family, rector and bishop. Neither the rector nor the bishop offered the young priest any signs of acceptance, encouragement or support, and his family rejected him. Three months later, the young priest was found murdered, stabbed repeatedly in the bedroom of the small house which the parish had provided for him.

"What can I do to help you?" she asked me. "I need to do something to help you as an attempt to assuage the guilt I feel for rejecting my own son when he needed me."

I asked her to be my friend, to pray for the soul of her son, to pray for me and other gays, to pray for our families, and to join me in saying yes to love, responsibility and justice; and no to guilt, no to alienation, no to disease, no to seduction, no to domination, no to duplicity, no to silence, no to invisibility, no to fear, no to humiliation, no to pious rhetoric, no to rigidity, no to repression, no to rejection, no to exile, no to violence, no to suicide, no to murder.

Thank you for your account of Mark's visit to Athens, especially for your hilarious description of his Vienna lover who sounds, by the way, like a real jerk. I received a card from Mark the other day, and he wrote how much he appreciated your and Minos' hospitality. I made my airline reservations last week and plan to be with you the last two weeks in August. Mark wants me to visit him in Vienna, but I'm not up to bickering with him, and would rather spend the time relaxing with you.

With my love,
Zal

✍

Southern Pines, NC
June 23, 1985

Dear Stephen,

You must be weary of my carrying on like this, but
you're the only one who can inspire me to keep my
courage. Then, when you were still teaching at school the
other night, poor Minos had to put up with me. All day
long, I try to act cool and calm, but then I come home
late each night and start screaming and throwing things,
and I need to talk with you. I should have allowed you to
make the trip over, but I think I can handle this if only
you will continue to listen lovingly to me and respond
with your customary gentleness, reserve and wisdom.
Please know that I don't mean to take any of my anger
and frustration out on you. Sam has forbidden me to let
anyone know about my sister's letter and my meeting
with the bishop, but I want to tell everyone, I want
everyone to know the humiliating circumstances a gay
candidate for the priesthood must suffer. My parishioners
would not stand for me to be treated this way. They need
to know the full story.

Two weeks ago yesterday, I was having lunch with
my parents at their house when the phone rang. It was
Sam, and his voice sounded unreal, unusually tense and
angry.

"Zal," he said, "I need to see you in my office."

"What's the matter?" I asked.

"Nothing much, except your ordination may be out
the window," he said. "I received a certified letter from
your sister, Dorothy, stating that you are a practicing
homosexual. And what's worse, she has sent copies to

both Bishop Estill and Bishop Moodey."

I started to laugh, which upset Sam even more. You see, I had signed for my sister's letter that morning in the office without realizing that it was from her. I had talked with Dorothy earlier that week when she had called to say that she was opposed to my ordination. We talked at length about my homosexuality and qualifications for the priesthood. She kept quoting Scriptural passages to me, all the while saying how much she loved me and was praying that I would "find the Lord." I made it clear that I intended to go ahead with my ordination, and that if she felt so strongly against it, she and her husband did not need to attend the service.

Not only did they not plan to attend, but Dorothy proceeded to write this formal protest, which included the statement, "After ordination, my brother intends to seek a lover." Sam really appreciated that line! Before I left my parents, I explained to them what had happened, and they had heard nothing of Dorothy's plans to write such a letter. In fact, they still expected Peter and her to attend the ordination.

Sam was beside himself when I met with him that afternoon.

"What has been going on?" he asked.

"It's simple," I said. "My sister is a charismatic Episcopalian, and she felt compelled to write in protest of my ordination."

"But what's all this business about being a practicing homosexual and seeking a lover after ordination?" he asked.

"I've had lovers, but I have never had to actively 'seek' a lover," I explained. "I am, however, always open to God leading me into a relationship with another man."

"But I thought you were dealing with all this in therapy," he said.

"Dealing with what, Sam? I'm in therapy in order to be a more effective pastor, not as a means of repressing my sexuality."

"What about now? Are you seeing anyone? Are you attracted to any men in this parish?"

I know I should have said that it was none of his business, but I couldn't resist sharing the names of many parishioners to whom I was attracted, and I watched while Sam's eyes widened in horror and disbelief.

"And Sam, are you attracted to any women in this parish?" I asked.

He was not amused, but insisted that I cancel my travel plans (I had been looking forward to attending a week-long youth leaders conference in western North Carolina) and await the deliberations of the bishop.

"What deliberations?" I asked. "Surely Bishop Estill won't refuse to ordain me at this stage."

"I wouldn't bet on it," he said.

"Sam, you can't let my sister's letter interfere with my ordination," I said. "You will support me in this, won't you?"

"I'll do all that I can," he said. "But as a priest, I owe my obedience to the bishop and will have to abide by his decision."

"How could he possibly refuse to ordain me?" I asked. "Why, the parish would be in an uproar if suddenly it was announced that my ordination was postponed."

"You keep all of this to yourself," he ordered. "I don't want you to breathe a word about this to anyone, do you understand? You know the Church canons, Zal. They clearly place your ordination in jeopardy."

"Baloney. The Church has no clear canon on the ordination of gays," I said. "In the absence of such, there is a resolution which many bishops have repudiated in recent years."

I then described the Church resolution covering the 'appropriate' sexual lifestyle for ministry to Sam. As you are well aware, those 1979 guidelines, still in effect, state:

— There are many human conditions, some in the area of sexuality, which bear upon a person's suitability for ordination.

— Every ordinand is expected to lead a life which is "a wholesome example to all people."

— Church leaders reaffirm the traditional teaching of the Church on marriage, marital fidelity, and sexual chastity as the standard of Christian sexual morality. Candidates for ordination are expected to conform to this standard. Therefore, Church leaders believe it is not appropriate for this Church to ordain a practicing homosexual, or any person who is engaged in heterosexual relations outside of marriage.

After the '79 resolution passed, a group of 23 bishops submitted a dissenting statement saying, "We do not believe that either homosexual orientation as such, nor the responsible and self-giving use of such a mode of sexuality, constitutes a scandal in and of itself."

Those who signed the statement expressed gratitude for "the profoundly valuable ministries of ordained persons, known to us to be homosexual, formerly and presently engaged in the service of this Church." The dissenting bishops stated that the '79 resolution carried with it "a cruel denial of the sexual beings of homosexual persons." They added that the action also condemned "countless lay persons of homosexual orientaion who are rendered second class citizens, fit to receive all other sacraments but the grace of Holy Orders, unless, in a sacrifice not asked of heterosexual persons generally, they abandon all hope of finding human fulfillment, under God, in a sexual and supportive relationship."

I'm beginning to think that what I am trying to do, i.e., respond to God's call to ordination, is impossible and that if any kind of balance, any kind of equilibrium is to be achieved in my life, I should probably sever all ties with the institutional Church. I am tired of being treated like the sick younger brother of the Church, I am tired of being told that I require the services of a psychiatrist because I happen to be gay. I've worked hard to get where I am, and now that ordination seems so near, I'm suddenly feeling that I could care less about it.

My meeting later that week with Bishop Estill was, I thought, much more relaxed than my meeting with Sam. When the bishop asked me if my sister's letter was true, I replied:

"It is true in the sense that I am gay, but I am not practicing at this time. I have been involved in a relationship with a man, and I am open to God leading me into another relationship, but my sister is wrong in writing that I am actively 'seeking' a lover. I'm sorry you had to learn about my homosexuality from my sister. I had wanted to tell you myself, but because so many people discouraged me from doing so, and primarily because of my own lapse of courage, I decided against it."

Bishop Estill made it clear that if I ever decided to live with a man in Southern Pines, he would have to remove me from the parish. He stated not once, but three times, that married priests are called to fidelity and single priests are called to celibacy. Period. The issue that seems to trouble Bishop Moodey of Ohio, Bishop Estill and Sam does not concern my homosexuality, but rather, the fact that I choose to function responsibly as an avowed gay priest. In other words, they accept my homosexuality *qua* my state of being but condemn homosexual acts. This dichotomy is false and serves the political expediency of disempowering the radical potential of my priesthood. It makes me 'safe' — oh, it's all right if you're gay, as long as you don't do anything about it.

Bishop Estill is quite sincerely amazed and overwhelmingly concerned that anyone aspiring to the office of a priest would, manifestly and explicitly, espouse a cultural position contrary to most of those with whom I am expected to relate pastorally. Furthermore, this contrariness is not merely his individual prejudice, but involves the issues of Church discipline, policy, condonement, implied sanction, etc., etc., ad nauseum. Thus, the bishop's concern about my ordination is not over how hard I have worked at the parish or whether I am adequately skilled, but over the personal package that I have, with my sister's letter serving as catalyst, confessed to him.

In theory, Bishop Estill's position has nothing to do with my personal convictions, their validity or his agreement or disagreement with them. He probably believes that his concern is over what God expects him to do about this case in North Carolina at this time, given the conservative attitudes of the diocesan clergy and lay leaders. For too long the Church has refused to recognize the obvious element of homosexuality among its priests and its communicants. My appearance in this diocese contrasts sharply with the cautious politicians and low-Church evangelicals, with their related commitments to the status quo.

Stephen, the Church desperately needs people like us who are broadly trained, yet can focus on specialized areas of ministry. The trouble with most Episcopal priests is that they are bland, upper middle-class, unfocused and insecure about their vocations and unwilling to passionately commit themselves to married people, singles, gays, the differently-abled, ecological sanity, peace, anti-nuclear activity or much of anything. We clergy are content to go to our meetings, pass our resolutions, keep quiet and hope our parishes will continue to pay our salaries.

After talking at length with Bishop Moodey and my sister, Bishop Estill, on behalf of the Bishop of Ohio, will proceed with my ordination next Sunday. Sam considers the bishop's decision to be a great blessing, and gushed on and on about how grateful I should be. It is sadly ironic, though, that I should feel compelled to be grateful for what is, in reality, just a begrudging and partial recognition of my rights as a gay person, glad for the crumbs thrown my way when others feast. I realize that I risk jeopardizing even that small dole when I demand full tolerance.

In the midst of all this, one of my AIDS patients named Roger, a 33-year-old former Marine from Southern Pines, died. His mother, a middle-aged widow named Mrs. Davis, lives alone in a small apartment, and never once visited her dying son in the hospital. When I arrived at her apartment the evening of his death, she was drunk and hostile toward me. When she began crying, I reached out and embraced her, and spent all night sitting with her on her couch. She cried most of the night, but occasionally would stop and share some memories of her only son.

I'm exhausted, and have been walking around in a daze. Everyone is so excited about next Sunday night's ordination. The choir has been working hard on the music. An outdoor reception under lights is being planned. I have no more desire to be a priest. I've lost patience with the hypocrisy, the cruelty of Church leaders who themselves are so numb they cannot hope to feel another person's pain. We priests are so concerned about spiritual power and control that we have become spiritually bankrupt and sexual imbeciles. Religious leaders today find themelves wallowing in a sea of decadence, with an inability to creatively use and understand their emotions, and with an exaggerated idolization of materiality and cheap gimmickry — precisely, I believe, because Church leaders have failed to give people what God gave us in Jesus, the Word made Flesh — incarnation and integration.

Why should I agree to be ordained a priest when Bishop Estill refuses to affirm me in my entirety as a gay man? I am understandably angry at a denomination that will tacitly accept my services, and even ordain me, without admitting publicly that it is doing so to a gay man. What will it take for Bishop Estill to truly acknowledge my presence as a priest, to recognize that the gay and lesbian community needs its representatives at the altar just as much as women and persons of color need theirs? Communicants throughout the diocese need also to see the diversity of the members of Christ's body.

Sam and the bishop have no power over me. Their

authority is null and void on account of their sheer stupidity. I will not allow them to dampen the spirit of my ordination. My ordination to the priesthood will take place next week, not because some homophobic bishop reluctantly lays his hands upon my head, but because the sacrament will represent a solemn covenant of mutual support, concern and trust, variations of which I experience from my parishioners each day as a deacon at Emmanuel.

With my love,
Zal

🎝

Southern Pines, NC
July 20, 1985

Dear Stephen,

I am feeling discouraged and am badly in need of my vacation with you. My days are numbered as a priest at Emmanuel Church. Time is running out. I feel like a man whose lover is about to abandon him for being unfaithful. I am not so afraid of what might happen to me, but I am concerned about the reputation of my parents, that they, Sam, and my Emmanuel friends will suffer because of my actions.

The ordination was splendid. Friends from Boston and Ohio arrived late that afternoon. My heart was liberated by the beauty of the church, decorated in candlelight and flowers. Joyful parishioners and friends crowded the church. The music was gloriously evocative of fire, love, passion, peace, eternal life.

After the service and reception, I hosted a party for my gay friends, my single friends, and out-of-town guests.

I was conscious of shaking throughout the party, and finally had to excuse myself and go to bed, even though I wanted to stay up and talk longer with friends whom I had not seen for many months. The party continued late into the night while I lay shivering beneath my covers. Seven friends spent the night at my house, and I left them sleeping the next morning while I walked to the parish for a staff meeting, which Sam insisted on calling, even though he knew I had out-of-town guests.

Sam asked me to remain following the staff meeting, and told me that he had received a phone call from Bishop Estill. The bishop had called to express his concern "that so many fairies were present at your ordination," said Sam.

I felt as if someone had kicked me in the stomach.

"They are my friends. I invited them," I said. "Why was the bishop so concerned?"

"He's afraid there will be an effort to appoint you chaplain of Integrity," Sam said. "He and I are both afraid that such an appointment would interfere with your parish work."

"I think I can be the judge of that," I said. "Did the bishop have anything to say about granting me canonical residence in this diocese?"

"Zal, we were lucky to even get you ordained," he said. "I doubt the bishop will go any further than that."

"Does this mean I should begin looking for work in another diocese?" I asked.

"That probably wouldn't be such a bad idea," Sam said.

"That's wonderful," I said. "Less than twelve hours after being ordained to the priesthood, I learn that I should begin circulating my resume. Why can't you help me,

Sam? Why don't you and the vestry insist that the bishop receive me as a voting member of the clergy of this diocese?"

"We've supported you all along, but I will not bring the vestry into a matter pertaining to your homosexuality," said Sam. "I've worked hard to build a decent vestry, and I will not allow your personal issues to split it apart. Besides, we have little influence when it comes to granting you canonical residence."

I was speechless. Why was Sam saying these things? Why isn't he willing to support me even though he knows how much I love him and the parish? Why is he so afraid of challenging the bishop and members of the parish vestry? What is he afraid of? Do you suppose he is hiding in his own kind of closet?

"One more thing," he said. "You need to be aware, Zal, that several prominent clergy have spoken with me, and have expressed concern about certain effeminate characteristics you have occasionally exhibited in public. We're afraid you will only hurt your chances of finding a job."

I left his office and spent most of that week entertaining my friends. I wanted to forget about Sam, forget about Emmanuel, forget about the Episcopal Church to which I had devoted my life. One night that week, my friends and I traveled to Durham for an Integrity meeting, during which I celebrated my first Eucharist and preached a homily on Deuteronomy 15:11 — "For the poor will never cease out of the land; therefore, I command you, you shall open wide your hand to your sister and brother, to the needy and the poor in the land." The following is an excerpt from that homily:

"The misery and oppression of poverty are experienced by lesbians and gay men who, because of their sexual orientation and their openness about that, face daily economic discrimination. When we are closeted about our homosexuality, we often attain certain measures of success, such as landing a prestigious job or living in an apartment that could be featured in an issue of *Architectural Digest*. But when God calls us to proclaim our homosexuality, we experience nightmares of losing our jobs and being evicted from our homes.

"I am suggesting that, unless we participate actively in the rebellion against those social structures and economic organizations which condemn openly gay men and lesbians to poverty, humiliation and degradation, then our spirituality will become irrelevant, and our religion will degenerate into a set of superstitions accepted by the fearful. Unless this chapter of Integrity expresses God's love for humanity by involvement and leadership in constructive protest against economic discrimination, then it will die, and will deserve to die.

"Our world is not one. Its people are more divided now, and also more conscious of their divisions, than they have ever been. They are divided between those who are satiated and those who are hungry. They are divided between those who are straight and those who are gay. They are divided between those who dominate and those who are dominated, between those who exploit and those who are exploited.

"As members of Integrity, we are to be not only the recipients of hope, but the givers of hope. We are to contribute our material resources that we may give hope to others — hope for our suffering lesbian sisters and gay brothers, hope for the hungry, hope for the needy, hope for the desperate. The source of that giving is God. God was rich, but God became poor for us. Therefore, as ministers, all of us are called to give and give again as God has given us."

Along that line, this past week my youth group and I completed a social outreach project in Northfork, West Virginia, an area that has suffered for about three-quarters of a century from the effects of coal mining. It is an area that faces persistently high unemployment. The dwindling population consists of a mixture of blacks, whites, miners and mountain folks, all of whom suffer from inadequate food, shelter and clothing.

I saw a pervading sense of gloom and hopelessness in the faces of the Appalachian jobless, who experience constant stress that often leads them to alcoholism, prostitution, theft, violence and suicide. Their children are barefoot and covered with soot from playing in slag piles, because there is not enough open space near their homes and schools for playgrounds. Coal dust fills the air, the residential sewage drips from rusty pipes into the town's only stream.

The poverty of Appalachia, the powerlessness, destitution and mental anguish of the poor of this region cry out to be redressed. Our group from Emmanuel responded not only by serving the poor and healing the brokenhearted, but by embracing poverty ourselves. We were constantly confronted with the question of whether the rich can help the poor in ways that maintain dignity and foster independence. We were not there to act as slaves to town residents, but rather, we came to be servants who took seriously the experience of the people we served.

We visited elderly persons, delivered groceries and daily meals to shut-ins, painted two houses and

constructed a room addition to a house. We lived in a
house in the neighborhood of the people we served. As a
community, we ate simple meals together, met regularly
for prayer, Bible study and song, and reflected each
evening on the day's events.

Our theology of ministry was born of a certain
humility and willingness to set aside the fixed
assumptions and comforts of our Southern Pines style of
life in the interest of serving the people of Northfork. The
outcome was something more valuable than the fruits of
gratuitous charity. It was genuine human solidarity.

Sometimes it was hard for me to sustain caring for
these people, to maintain a sense of hope and purpose, or
a wish for improvement when their circumstances were
so grim. I was hot and tired from painting one afternoon,
so I sat down on the ground. Before long, I felt a tap on
my shoulder, and the elderly woman who owned the
house offered me a cup of cold water. It then dawned on
me that these poor persons were as concerned for us as we
were for them. My heart was changed forever.

After I reported on our Northfork trip to Sam, he
asked, "Do you think you will take a group to Appalachia
next year?" I looked puzzled, then said, "But it was my
understanding that I would not be here next year since my
contract expires at the end of June."

"Nonsense," he said. "You can stay at Emmanuel for
three to five years if you want, and simply remain
canonically resident of Ohio. Who cares if you're not
canonically resident of North Carolina, as long as you can
continue working on our staff?"

"I care," I said. "If I can't have a voice and a vote on
Church issues like every other priest in North Carolina,
then I cannot continue serving the diocese in my capacity

as a priest at Emmanuel. I want canonical residence, and I deserve it."

"Well, we can't always get what we want," Sam snapped.

I recently decided to write an essay on my theology of ministry from my perspective as a gay priest, and have submitted it to the *Witness*, an ecumenical journal of social concern. Their September issue will focus on AIDS and homophobia in the Church. I've enclosed a copy for your perusal. The *Witness* editor is concerned that I might lose my job if she publishes the essay, but as you can see, there is nothing in the essay that could be deemed objectionable. As for possible repercussions resulting from its publication — I doubt my parishioners will ever read it, as the *Witness'* circulation is not that widespread. I'm primarily addressing gay seminarians, clergy and bishops in the essay.

With my love,
Zal

❧

"On being a gay priest"
by Zalmon O. Sherwood
From the *Witness*,
September, 1985

"We're concerned about you," a priest friend pulls me aside and whispers in my ear. "Go ahead and be gay, but for God's sake, be discreet."

Barely two months have passed since I, a gay man, was ordained a priest. Why do I qualify myself as a gay man at the beginning of this essay? Many of my friends and colleagues discourage me from proclaiming my homosexuality. They consider it a private, personal characteristic, one that, if publicly known, would interfere with my capacity to minister to people.

"I want you to be successful," my friend continues. "I want you to attain a level of power that will make it possible for you to do great things for the Church and society."

"Be patient," advised my former spiritual director. "Wait a while longer before flaunting your homosexuality. In fact, why flaunt it at all? Jesus never dwelled on his sexual preference."

Of course my friends, both gay and straight, are concerned, even afraid. I'm afraid myself at times. But their fear is massive and supported by the homophobic conviction that coming out is "not worth it," which is to say, "I'm not worth it."

I have come to accept and love this particular person who I am and the spiritual journey which is my own. In coming out, my life and ministry become a public witness of homosexual Christian maturity and a gift to the next generation. Such a witness is generative because it provides a publicly observable model of how God can act in the life of a gay person.

Most of my gay friends were raised in a milieu of social intolerance so pervasive that at times, even today, it still seems natural. How is it possible for any of us to escape entirely the homophobia that was an inextinguishable presence throughout our formative years and whose scars we bear today? We learned in our homes, schools and churches that homosexuality is a sin, an aberration, that our homosexual feelings are unnatural and shameful. And so our feelings were repressed, punished and closeted. If we dare to live openly gay lives, we are, more often than not, excluded, despised, slandered, robbed of human rights. Yes, our souls are scarred, and it is not surprising that so many gay persons see only the scars and mistake them for their whole selves, hating in themselves and thus in others that which can lead to a more meaningful life, if recognized and affirmed as a gift from God.

My 'coming out' is a rejection of the images of hetero-sexuality that society expects from me. By being both honest with myself and others, I am being honest with God, and therefore more open to God's grace. Being an avowed gay priest leads me to a deeper and more vulnerable, more compassionate sense of belonging with others who suffer unjustly. God calls me to be in solidarity with other oppressed minorities, and to demand with them and for them social justice and civil rights.

What God had fashioned within and around me, i.e., my homosexuality, is precisely that which calls me to the ministry. My heart, my soul, my voice respond to God's call, because I see all too clearly the pain and suffering, not only of my life, but in the lives of people who come to me for prayer and counsel. In order to grow spiritually, I have had to acknowledge, then let go of the pain, the betrayal, the guilt, so that I can proceed to follow Christ and be a channel of his healing and reconciling powers. As a minister, I am called to encounter all persons as human equals with understanding and sensitivity, and thus free persons from stereotypes and cultural prejudice.

We all want to be open and authentic, to be freely ourselves and accepted as such. Yet gay persons know that much of what they legitimately want in life may elude them if they are open about their homosexuality. I often

experience a sense of spiritual homelessness that results
from trying to work gracefully in what is largely a hostile
environment. It is a dangerous struggle in which I am
engaged, that of disillusionment with the institutional
Church of which I choose to be a part.

I remain in the Church, because I remember that
Jesus' disciples consisted of those persons outside the
traditional, established centers of social and economic
power. The Church today will thrive only to the degree
that it embraces, in their full humanity, those persons on
the margins of life.

My own experience of marginalization empowers me
to reach out to others at the edges of society — battered
women, abused children, prisoners, refugees, mentally
and physically differently-abled persons, poor and hungry
persons, elderly persons, persons of color and different
faiths. I shall always live at the margins, at times closer,
at times farther from the centers of social, religious and
political life.

As a gay priest, I do not attempt to disguise my
homosexuality behind the disembodied prestige of the
clerical collar. I am committed to seeking ways to heal
the division between body and soul, which means helping
people to realize that God is deeply enmeshed in our most
ordinary daily lives, instead of located in some other-
worldly, transcendent, never-never land. By remaining
silent about my homosexuality, I am prevented from
describing my intimate relationships, and hence come
across as incapable of forming any. In our silence, in the
secrets and lies we cling to, we are stripping our vocations
of any passion and integrity.

ᔥ

Priest's homosexuality a dilemma for Episcopalians

by Diane Winston
(from *The Raleigh News & Observer*,
September 29, 1985)

A parish priest in the affluent community of Southern Pines, the Rev. Zalmon O. Sherwood has all the right stuff.

An accomplished musician, he related well as a deacon and later as an assistant priest to young people and singles at Emmanuel Episcopal Church. Soft-spoken and genteel, he mixed comfortably with the flock. He won the parish tennis tournament and played a good game of golf.

Earlier this month, Zal Sherwood stunned the staid and sedate Southern Pines community by revealing that he is gay. He declared his homosexuality in an article, "On being a gay priest," that he wrote for the current issue of the *Witness*, a denominational magazine.

"In coming out, my life and ministry become a public witness of homosexual Christian maturity and a gift to the next generation," Sherwood wrote.

"Coming out" also may cost him his job. Although he wants to stay, Sherwood wonders whether the parish will support him.

In declaring his homosexuality, Sherwood forced state Episcopal leaders to confront an issue — whether gays should be ordained — that has wracked most mainline Protestant denominations for the past decade.

With the birth of the gay rights movement in the 1960s, homosexuals began agitating for acceptance in all sectors of society. Although most denominations have affirmed the concept of "gay rights" — non-discriminatory treatment of homosexuals in housing and employment — the question of ordaining them to the ministry has proved particularly controversial.

Most opponents base their argument on the Bible. Sodom and Gomorrah, cities where homosexuality was widespread, were destroyed because of their residents' wickedness, according to Genesis 18:1-19, 29. In Leviticus 18:22, men are told not to have sex with other men. The New Testament in general appears to condemn homosexuality, specifically in Romans 1:18-32, in which Paul describes homosexuality as a sin that has made God angry.

Heterosexuality, say proponents of this view, is the God-given and normal expression of human sexuality.

But a clamorous minority of churchgoers disagrees. Transcending specific biblical injunctions, they say, is the Christian ethic of love God loves all creation, of which homosexuals are a part, these churchgoers say.

Adherents of this view cite current research in the social sciences which claims that homosexuality is an inherent condition of a small percentage of the population.

Sherwood's article appeared during the denomination's triennial conference in Anaheim, California, this month. Among the surprised readers was the Rt. Rev. Robert W. Estill, bishop of the Diocese of North Carolina and the man who ordained Sherwood.

"He didn't tell me he was gay," said Estill, when asked whether he knew about Sherwood's sexuality before his ordination. "He said he was uncertain about his sexuality, but he would never do anything to bring attention to himself, the Church or Emmanuel Parish."

Estill, whose diocese reaches from Rocky Mount to Charlotte, said in an interview that he "would not knowingly ordain a person who was a practicing homosexual."

He based his stance on a 1979 resolution by Episcopal bishops discouraging ordination of gay men and lesbians.

The resolution affirmed the "mystery of human sexuality" and recognized "that homosexuals are children of God." But it also stated, "We believe it is not appropriate for this Church to ordain a practicing homosexual, or any person who is engaged in heterosexual relations outside of marriage."

Later in the 1979 convention, 23 bishops released a statement repudiating the resolution.

"We have no intention of ordaining irresponsible persons," the bishops wrote. "But we do not believe that either homosexual orientation as such, nor the responsible and self-giving use of such a mode of sexuality, constitutes a scandal in and of itself."

Among the statement's signers was the Rt.

Rev. Edmond L. Browning, bishop of Hawaii. This year in Anaheim, Browning was elected presiding bishop of the 2.8 million-member denomination. After his election, when asked about ordaining homosexuals, Browning side-stepped the issue. But he reiterated his support for gay rights.

The issue of homosexual priests resurfaced in other forums at the Anaheim gathering.

The House of Bishops passed a resolution saying, "No one should be denied access to the ordination process in this Church because of race, color, ethnic origin, gender, sexual orientation, physical handicap or age except as otherwise specified by canon."

Subsequently, the measure was killed in a close vote by lay delegates to the denomination's House of Deputies. Clergy delegates passed the resolution.

Two North Carolinians who were present at that meeting said they opposed ordaining gays.

"I think the current statement the Church has is fine," said Scott T. Evans of Durham. "It's not the norm at this time."

"If I were a bishop, I'd not knowingly ordain one," said Joseph B. Cheshire Jr., a Raleigh lawyer whose grandfather was a bishop of the Diocese of North Carolina. "I just think there are certain characteristics people have that make them less suitable for the ministry."

Sherwood, 28, who came to Emmanuel in the summer of 1984, said last week that his sexual preference had little to do with his fitness for

the ministry. Acknowledging his homosexuality, he said in an interview, enabled him to
serve as a role model for other homosexuals.

"As a gay priest, it is important for me to
help lesbians and gay men learn what it means to
be able to recognize and accept themselves as
God's children, who are fully entitled to love
responsibly, without hiding and without guilt,"
said Sherwood, a graduate of Episcopal Divinity
School in Cambridge, Massachusetts.

But he also had another agenda — fighting
what he perceived as discrimination.

A native of Ohio, Sherwood had been accepted for ordination by the Rt. Rev. James R.
Moodey, the bishop of the Diocese of Ohio. Because Sherwood was working in North Carolina
at the time, Moodey asked Estill to ordain him.
After the ordination, Sherwood sought to have
his canonical residency (church affiliation)
changed from Ohio to North Carolina, which
would place him under Estill's jurisdiction.
Estill refused the request.

"He's withholding it from me because he
considers it inappropriate for a priest to identify
with the gay community and be an advocate of
gay rights," said Sherwood, who said his article
in the *Witness* was part of the fight against
discrimination.

Estill agreed that the factor entered into his
decision, but he said the primary reason was a
letter he received from Sherwood's sister two
weeks before Sherwood's ordination in June.

"His sister wrote that he was gay and

planned to get a lover if ordained," Estill said.

Estill said he then asked Sherwood about his sexual orientation. "He came to me and said he was uncertain about his sexuality but was open to, one day, getting a lover."

Sherwood's answer persuaded Estill to ordain him, but Estill said he withheld canonical residency "because for his own good he needed to be closely related to those people . . . in Ohio, who passed on him and knew him better than the people here."

Sherwood recalls the incident differently. Describing his sister as a "fundamentalist and charismatic" Episcopalian, he said she wrote to Estill expressing her distress at the ordination.

"Estill said, 'What does this mean?'" Sherwood said. "I said, 'I'm gay, but not practicing at this time.'"

Sherwood said that was his standard reply whenever he was asked about his sexuality. But he said he rarely was asked.

"There were many opportunities for me to be a lot more honest with Church leaders, but the pressure was great to remain silent," he said. "The basic issue is — am I less of a priest because I happen to be gay?"

For Estill, the answer is yes.

"I'm an advocate of gay rights and civil rights for all persons," he said. "But to be an active proponent of gay lifestyles and a focus of one's ministry seems inappropriate for an ordained priest."

Estill added that at this point, a majority of bishops judged an active homosexual lifestyle to fall short of the exemplary and Godly behavior required of clergy.

Cheshire, an active layman, said he believed the Church had a ministry to homosexuals but should not ordain them.

"I don't want to come down appearing to be a Jerry Falwell fundamentalist, but I'm thinking about the best ministry of the Church overall," he said. "Most people would prefer not to have their children supervised by people of that caste."

According to Sherwood, many lesbians and gay men already have been ordained — some are celibate, others are married. But unlike him, they choose to remain silent.

"Zal would argue that the Church makes you go underground," Estill said. "It's a fine point whether a person can be gay and celibate and a person who is a proponent of it, a spokesman and eventually an active, practicing homosexual."

Estill said the experience has made him wary of ordaining priests who have not been under the wing of his diocese. And although Sherwood would have to leave the diocese when his two-year residency ended next summer, Estill said he hoped that Emmanuel Parish would deal with its young minister "pastorally."

Although Sherwood said he had received support from many parishioners, he said Friday that he might be pressured to leave Emmanuel.

"I pray that the parish will look at the quality of my ministry and the quality of my life, and realize that my ministry to gays is just a part of that," he said. "God created gay people, too. They should be entitled to a full ministry."

But the Rev. Samuel C. Walker, Sherwood's rector at Emmanuel, refused to comment on his assistant's future at the parish.

"It takes a lot of courage to do what he's done," Walker said, adding that he would say no more. "I admire him for that."

✖

Rector's weekly message on Sunday bulletin
September 29, 1985
Emmanuel Episcopal Church
Southern Pines, NC

Dear Friends,

There are great blessings in living in a free society. Freedoms are guaranteed by law which enable ideas and information to be expressed. A free press is one of these and we should always be grateful for the news that's "fit to print." It keeps us informed of daily life around the world. Even when some of the news is disturbing or makes us bristle, we may remain objective and keep an open mind by remembering some things.

First, what we read is at best part of the whole story and interpreted through the eyes and mind of one reporter. Accuracy can be blurred.

Second, "sensationalism" is no substitute for journalism but it does sell newspapers, often at the expense of innocent people. Reactions from shock or fear are not healthy or productive.

Finally, the freedom of the press, like that of an individual, must be balanced by responsibility which is vital to the media's ministry for the common good. When that's missing, we're reading half-truths and may judge accordingly.

The Episcopal Church is "in the news" because we've had a convention, elected a presiding bishop, and acted on some issues. Quotes and reports on this and that can be misleading and confusing. The real work of your Church begins at this altar and in the daily life of this parish community. Where Christ reigns there is love and truth, freedom and responsibility.

Sincerely,
The Rev. Samuel C. Walker,
Rector

❧

Remarks to Senior High Youth Group
by Zalmon O. Sherwood
September 29, 1985
Emmanuel Episcopal Church
Southern Pines, NC

I'm sorry we had to call this special meeting tonight, and I'm grateful to all of you who could attend at such short notice. It has been a wild week at Emmanuel, and this group has especially been on my mind.

Mr. Walker is going to mail a letter tomorrow to each member of the congregation. In it, he will announce that I have resigned from the staff and will soon be moving from Southern Pines. I wanted to meet with you tonight to discuss the reasons why I must leave, to answer any questions you may have, and to begin the process of saying good-bye

Many weeks ago, I made a decision to write an article which was published in a magazine called the *Witness*, a journal that is primarily read by Episcopal clergy. In the article, I wrote about being a gay priest. You need to try to understand that when I tell you that I am gay, I am referring not only to my sexuality. When I tell you that I am gay, I am identifying with a minority of persons whose basic human rights and dignity are often violated if they choose to live openly gay lives.

Because of all the publicity ensuing from the *Witness* article, Bishop Estill, Mr. Walker and the leaders of this parish consider it inappropriate for me to continue functioning as a priest in Southern Pines. They have asked me to stop my advocacy work for gay rights in North Carolina, but I am unwilling to stop. God calls you and me to identify with all oppressed minorities — gay persons, persons of color, prisoners, poor and elderly persons — and to assist them in obtaining social justice and civil rights.

I believe God is also calling me to be with you. I've enjoyed being with you and have always looked forward to our times together. In fact, I love you. But you're old enough to realize that we can't always get what we want, so I have had to make a choice, a decision to minister to persons less fortunate than you and I.

Before I end, I need to ask you two things. First, whenever you meet together as a group, or if you're in church on Sunday, will you please say a prayer for me, because I'm feeling afraid of about what the future holds for me. And when I move, I plan to take a list with all your names on it, and I'm going to pray every day for each one of you, because I know that many of you must also be feeling afraid, or angry, or betrayed, or confused, or a combination of all sorts of feelings. I will pray also that our paths might cross someday, and I will let you know where I am living.

The second thing I'm going to ask is that you continue meeting as a group, and that you love each other when you are together or apart. Love each other and take care of each other. Love your adult advisors, and advisors, love these special young persons. Love Mr. Walker, love this parish, and most important of all, love God, because God is the source of all love.

❧

Letter sent to parishioners
Emmanuel Episcopal Church,
Southern Pines, NC
September 30, 1985

Dear Friends,

Zalmon Sherwood, during his brief tenure as an assistant on the clergy staff of Emmanuel Parish has, in fact, contributed greatly to the church's overall ministry. His responsibilities in program and pastoral matters have been faithfully discharged. His ministry with music has helped produce a superb offering.

It is with regret that we must accept his decision to make a public statement of his alignment with the homosexual community and his corresponding decision to resign from this staff in order to pursue a direction of ministry to that community. News of this has come as surprise and shock.

Since there is a need for priestly concern and counseling of the so-called "gay" society who are Episcopalians, Zalmon's decision necessitates his leaving this parish to pursue re-location through some other diocese to follow this ministry.

It is important that we give thanks for Zal's time among us, and look ahead with prayer to both his growing and our own.

While Zalmon is no longer on our staff he will remain for a time in our community and we trust that if you need to communicate personally with him you will find an appropriate way.

Your bishop, rector and vestry deeply regret the manner in which some of these events have happened, but we believe it is far healthier to live the truth than practice falsehood. We look for your continued prayers and support for the fine work of this parish community, that we all grow in grace.

Sincerely,
The Rev. Samuel C. Walker, Rector
John B. Evans, Senior Warden
Asbury Coward III, Junior Warden

✣

Letter to the Editor,
October 2, 1985
The *Pilot*,
Southern Pines, NC

To the Editor:

Last Sunday morning, following the 11 a.m. service at Emmanuel Episcopal Church, the rector of the parish made one of the most shocking announcements I have ever heard. The Rev. Zalmon O. Sherwood, one of four Emmanuel priests, had declared himself to be a homosexual and had resigned.

Tears flowed, and parishioners softly wept. It was a wrenching experience that won't go away.

Earlier, at the 9 a.m. service, Fr. Sherwood was not permitted to celebrate the Eucharist.

At this writing, 46 hours later, I have been unable to think of anything else. I feel sad, angry, bitter, disillusioned, betrayed.

As a member of the choir, which Fr. Sherwood directed, and as a member of the parish music committee, which he chaired, I have been privileged to know him for what he is — an extremely sensitive and hard-working cleric with nervous energy, who is held in adoration by young and old alike (not a common combination).

I know him as the most able and knowledgeable musician in the Sandhills. Veteran parishioners tell me they have never heard such exciting music at Emmanuel since Fr. Sherwood arrived less than two years ago.

He has made the modest 14-rank Wicks organ sound infinitely superior to what it sounds like in less capable hands. He has imported guest instrumentalists and other organists. Perhaps most importantly, he has introduced a growing and enthusiastic choir to an assortment of music that is both challenging and in the finest traditions of Anglican Church music.

There are a number of intriguing facets to this issue which require examination and assessment.

Few would quarrel with parents understandably fearful of the potential dangers inherent in the association of a gay priest with impressionable youths. One of the most distressing bits of information which have come to light is that no one at Emmanuel has even discussed changes in job description for its gay priest, which would isolate him from boys and girls.

This is an explosive and emotional issue. Several
things must be said to set the record straight.

1. Fr. Sherwood is a homosexual who champions the
civil rights of gays as members of God's family.

2. Fr. Sherwood is still under the jurisdiction of the
Diocese of Ohio. He asked for transfer of jurisdiction to
the Diocese of North Carolina, but the Rt. Rev. Robert W.
Estill, our bishop, rejected the request with the non-
convincing reason that Fr. Sherwood had a longer and
closer rapport with his peers in Ohio. In short, Bishop
Estill wanted no part of the Sherwood dilemma.

3. The effect of the bishop's non-action was to toss
the slippery ecclesiastical ball into Emmanuel's court.

4. Emmanuel's rector and vestry took the least
courageous of all possible alternatives. First, the vestry
said Fr. Sherwood could stay if he would cease and desist
from advocacy of gays. The priest refused this stick-and-
carrot approach with the explanation that his ministry
had to be all-inclusive.

5. Fr. Sherwood was asked by the rector to tender his
resignation "for the good of all concerned." No boat
rocking, please!

Fr. Sherwood does not now — nor did he ever — plan
to minister exclusively to the gay community.
Homosexuals are a small part of a much larger human
family, as he perceives it.

The words love, compassion, forgiveness and
understanding have saturated the sanctuary of Emmanuel
Church for the past few years. This hollow rhetoric has
made a sad mockery of what Jesus taught by example
when he faced up to the powerful religious leaders of his
day, called them hypocrites, and forgave a variety of
sinners — even street walkers.

Where does love and compassion and forgiveness and understanding begin, and where can you find it if it's not in church?

At the very least, the vestry should refuse to accept a resignation not voluntarily tendered.

A good deal of soul-searching went into this writing. I had to weigh the almost certain parish divisiveness which this issue has brought to Emmanuel, as opposed to the rights and human dignity of one 28-year-old priest.

And I have to look into the mirror every morning, knowing that I resent being part of a slickly-contrived lynching.

Donald C. Cressman
Whispering Pines, NC

✴

Letter to the Editor,
October 2, 1985
The *Pilot*,
Southern Pines, NC

To the Editor:

Will Rogers said that all he knew was what he read in the newspapers so he could, presumably, have drawn some rather far-reaching opinions from a front page article in the most recent edition of the Sunday *Raleigh News & Observer*. The article, "Priest's homosexuality a dilemma for Episcopalians," focused on a parish priest at Emmanuel Episcopal Church in Southern Pines.

It seems that this man's job is in jeopardy at Emmanuel Church because he openly declared his homosexuality in an article written for a denominational magazine. I, for one, would like to suggest that based on the information in the article, this man should not only be retained as a parish priest, he should also be given a raise.

According to the article, the rector at Emmanuel Church said, "It takes a lot of courage to do what he's done. I admire him for that." The Episcopal bishop of the Diocese of North Carolina said, "I'm an advocate of gay rights and civil rights for all persons." The current presiding bishop of the entire denomination is on record as having signed a statement which says, "We do not believe that either homosexual orientation as such, nor the responsible and self-giving use of such a mode of sexuality, constitutes a scandal in and of itself."

If these quotes are correct, what is the problem? His rector admires his courage for openly declaring his homosexuality. The head of the denomination for all of North Carolina is an advocate of gay rights (unless he is a hypocrite, this would include the right to employment). The head of the denomination for the entire nation believes that men having sex with men does not constitute a scandal in and of itself. What is the problem?

Although I was married in the Episcopal Church more than twenty years ago, the fact that I have since gotten saved and become an ignorant fundamentalist may have robbed me of my genteel sensitivity. I find myself unable to appreciate the incongruity of this entire scenario. Here is a man who asks nothing more than to be allowed to advocate publicly the practical implications of the positions espoused by the leaders of his denomination. It is time for Episcopalians to stop playing religious games and face facts.

You have a presiding bishop who believes that it is acceptable for men to have sex with men. You have a bishop of the Diocese of North Carolina who is a self-declared "advocate" (look up that word in the dictionary) of gay rights. To find a local reminder of the national problem and pretend that the problem is solved is a moral and spiritual absurdity.

The Bible declares unequivocally that homosexuality is an abomination in the sight of God (Leviticus 18:22; Leviticus 20:13; Romans 1:18-32; etc.). I oppose the firing of this homosexual priest for a practical reason — the more perversion is embraced by apostate denominations, the more clearly the lines will be drawn between those who are loyal to denominations, and those who are loyal to the Word of God.

As the pastor of some former Episcopalians, I am specifically aware that there are still men and women who reject the obvious hypocrisy of being taught the Word of God by people who do not believe the Word of God.

The Rev. Kent Kelly
Calvary Memorial Church
Southern Pines, NC

✿

Weekly message on Sunday bulletin
October 6, 1985
Emmanuel Episcopal Church,
Southern Pines, NC

Dear Friends,
    These have, I know, been difficult and painful days for all of you at Emmanuel Church and in the community

of Southern Pines. Your clergy and vestry and I have been in close touch and I want to use this bulletin to let you know of my continued prayers and concern.

It is my hope that we can all return to the work of the ministry our Lord has given us. Zal Sherwood is staying in touch with me and I have assured him of my eagerness to be a pastor to him at this time in his life and ministry.

I am proud of Sam Walker and of the manner in which he has conducted himself both as a rector and a pastor. He knows that he has my full support and confidence, and I feel that is true of each of you.

Faithfully,
The Rt. Rev. Robert W. Estill
The Bishop of North Carolina

✑

Letter from Integrity to Bishop Estill
October 7, 1985

Dear Bishop Estill:

First, we would like to offer you our thanks for supporting gay and lesbian issues at the General Convention. And we also appreciate your past and continuing support for the Triangle (Raleigh, Durham, Chapel Hill) Chapter of Integrity. We know that publicly taking these stands can be difficult for someone in your position, and so we are especially grateful. We believe that both of these decisions have gone a great way toward improving the health of the Church.

Now we are disturbed over recent actions taken against the Rev. Zalmon O. Sherwood. Your words of support are clearly heard, yet your absence is equally clearly felt. As members of Integrity who love the

Church, we are trying to quell our anger, our strong sense that an act of hypocrisy has taken place, our difficulty seeing Mr. Sherwood's forced resignation in any light other than this — the Episcopal Church of the Diocese of North Carolina, in the people of the Rev. Samuel C. Walker and the Rt. Rev. Robert W. Estill, does not really support gays.

We certainly hope this perception is incorrect and, to that end, would like you to clarify several points for us:

1. You stated when you met with us and also in the September 29 *Raleigh News & Observer* that "to be an active proponent of gay lifestyles and a focus of one's ministry seems inappropriate for an ordained priest." If you believe that gay men and lesbians have equality with all other members of your flock, then how can you support the above statement while allowing black priests in this diocese to advocate and actively seek increased civil rights for blacks?

2. Do you indeed believe that the homosexual persons of your diocese are as equal in the affairs of the Church and in the eyes of God as the heterosexual persons of your flock? Why or why not?

3. Aside from believing that Mr. Sherwood's support of gay rights is inappropriate, do you have any moral stand against him as a homosexual priest? Are there any other reasons that Mr. Sherwood is not suitable for the ordained ministry?

4. It is our understanding that you have refused on several occasions to accept Mr. Sherwood's Letter Dimissory from the Diocese of Ohio. Do you have any prejudicial reasons for not accepting him as a voting priest in the Diocese of North Carolina? If so, what are they?

5. You say that being a public proponent of gay issues

is inappropriate behavior for a member of the ordained ministry. We would like to know what type of support for gay men and lesbians you oppose and what type of support do you plan to propose (e.g., educational programs on human sexuality in general, homosexuality and AIDS in particular)? You have yourself supported some changes by your votes at General Convention. Is it support for change within the community which you find inappropriate?

6. "I would never knowingly ordain a person who is a practicing homosexual." How can you support this quote from the *News & Observer* and also be an advocate of gay rights? Are you saying that gay rights do not apply to the affairs of the Church?

By a virtually unanimous vote, the Triangle Chapter of Integrity has resolved to present you with the following statement:

We urge you to work actively to get Mr. Sherwood reinstated at Emmanuel Church. Realizing that a bishop cannot force a parish to accept a priest, if the above is not acceptable to the parish, we urge you to find some other position for him within the diocese. If a parish post is not available at this time we are urging you to appoint Mr. Sherwood to a diocesan staff position, preferably as a missioner to the lesbian and gay community.

Realizing that there are already several other gay priests within the diocese, we urge you to accept Mr. Sherwood's Letter Dimissory from the Diocese of Ohio. The very large community of gay Episcopalians within this diocese needs a Christian leader as a role model for our spiritual lives.

We believe that you should not criticize Mr. Sherwood for being called by God to function responsibly as an avowed gay priest. Attempting to force him into silence is tantamount to encouraging hypocrisy. Unless you actively support us in the person of Zalmon Sherwood you are allowing the sin of homophobia to flourish in this state. Your active support for gay issues would discourage violence and hatred against our gay and lesbian community.

This may be difficult for you as the leader of this diocese; however, the time has come for the Church to take an active positive stand for gays both in the Church and in the world. As the time came to see blacks and women as human beings worthy of serving God in all ways, so now the time has come for us. We, too, are children of God, ready to serve the whole Church, in love and gladness, to the glory of God.

Help us do that.

Triangle Chapter of Integrity
Durham, NC

❧

Statement of Bishop Estill's position
on lesbian and gay issues in the Church,
presented in response to the Integrity letter.
October 15, 1985
St. Joseph's Episcopal Church,
Durham, NC

I support our Church's official position that homosexual persons are children of God who have a full and equal claim with all persons upon the love, acceptance, and pastoral concern and care of the Church. Indeed, I support the rights of all people to access to all the benefits provided by the Christian Church generally, and the Episcopal Church in particular.

This does not, however, mean that all people are entitled to be ordained or to exercise priestly functions within the Church. No member of the Episcopal Church, however devoted, has a right to ordination, because that person feels a personal call to such ordination, however strong that subjective call may be. The Church, under its regulations, examines each applicant and sees that the applicant has the various qualifications to serve the entire Church as well as the necessary commitment.

Applicants must have obtained the consent of various committees and commissions of clergy and laity, as well as the willingness of the diocesan bishop to actually ordain him or her. The Church calls and ordains only those selected.

Under the regulations of the Church, every ordained person has a residence in the diocese in which he or she was originally ordained, or such other diocese to which they may subsequently transfer, with the permission of both the bishop in the original diocese and of the diocese to which they are transferred.

It is possible and not uncommon for a deacon or priest to be canonically resident in one diocese and work in another diocese. In such cases, the bishop of the diocese in which the deacon is physically located may have a specific request of the deacon's bishop to ordain the deacon to be a priest. It is simply a matter of logistics and does not confer upon the ordinand any special or different rights.

The Church does not require me as a bishop to ordain or to accept into canonical relationship with the Diocese of North Carolina any person whose presence in or connected with this diocese acting will not be in the best interest of the diocese.

As bishop of the Diocese of North Carolina, and in the interest of all people, it is my persuasion that I will not knowingly ordain or accept as a canonical resident a person, however well qualified otherwise, who is a practicing homosexual, or who, as a heterosexual, is engaged in relations outside of marriage. This is not my judgment of any such persons. It is simply my conclusion from what I believe is in the best interests of Christ's Church within the Diocese of North Carolina, and it is consistent with the actions of our national Church's General Convention.

❧

Southern Pines, NC
October 20, 1985

Dear Stephen,

I seem to be in the midst of one of those rare, and usually bittersweet *kairos* experiences, in which our God of justice shatters the defenses of those who would impede Her strong desire that all women and men be accorded respect and dignity. Minos was an angel to call the other night and insist that I return to Greece, and when I refused, he said he would send you over here. Yes, that is what I would love more than anything, to have you here by my side. But you must remain in Athens. Minos and your students need you. And for the time being, I am needed here. My gay brothers and lesbian sisters need me. We are striving, hungry for our rightful place in the world, yearning for much more than the begrudged tolerance the Church has given us.

Since my resignation several weeks ago, I have been thrust into the public light. I am not a faceless spokesperson, to be sure. The situation is particularly and uniquely mine, and the pain ultimately mine to suffer. But insofar as the opportunity this publicity brings me to make my voice heard inside and outside the Church is a collective one affecting the lives of many gay persons, I am not alone. "Collective" because it is founded on a history of the struggle for gay rights, without which I would have been ignored as well as exiled from the Church.

The day my resignation became effective, I was being interviewed by a Durham television reporter in the parish garden. It was twilight, the birds were singing and I was recounting the events leading up to my resignation. Suddenly Sam drove up in his car, interrupted the interview, refused to answer any of the reporter's questions, and pulled me aside.

"Zal," he whispered, "all the television stations are promoting interviews with the 'gay priest who was fired from his job.' You're getting in way over your head. You're being manipulated, exploited by members of the media and gay community. I don't want to see you getting hurt. Just think about how all this publicity will affect your parents. Think about how all the children will react."

I continued with the interview.

My heart is filled with sorrow and with shock at the horror of it all. This handling seems so archaic, so inhuman. Somewhere there is anger, but it gets diffused by incredulity. I cannot comprehend the insensitive, dark-ages mentality of Bishop Estill and Sam, who are responsible for my forced resignation.

I grieve for my loss, I grieve for my gay friends who

feel abandoned and discounted, I grieve for my parents who are understandably hurt and confused. Most of all, I grieve for my youth group. When I met with the youth group shortly after my resignation, I was feeling at peace and in control until I witnessed forty teenage boys and girls weeping from the shock of my announcement. It was then that I became aware of the great evil that was being done not only to me, but also to these young people, and especially to the gay and lesbian teenagers who are part of my youth group. Do Church officials suppose that silencing me will keep them from discovering their sexual orientation? Hardly. It only teaches them to hate themselves for what they are. Read the following excerpt from a letter written by Robert, a 15-year-old youth group member:

"No gay priests. What a stupid rule! All I know is that you're Zal and I love Zal and I don't want Zal to leave. I wake up each morning and keep hoping that it has all been a nightmare. Everybody at school admires you for what you've done. Blanche Slade, for example, even though she had come just two or three times to youth group, cried for you in front of everybody at school."

After firing me, Sam pleaded with me not to respond to press requests for interviews. He seemed so concerned about scandal, about tarnishing the image of his priesthood. His Nixonesque belief that truth cannot be uncovered and conscientiously communicated subverts and perverts the discipline of journalism. He finally agreed to two newspaper interviews, in which he (taking his cue from Bishop Estill) usurped the truth and replaced it with a self-serving version of events designed to discredit me and maintain the image of the Episcopal Church. In one account, not only does Sam attempt to discredit me by

denying both that he knew I was gay and that he had
forced my resignation, but he proceeds to portray me as
"an angry young man" and a deceitful publicity-seeker
"who cares about himself far above the Church, the
community, the people, even his own family."

I fail to understand why some people persist in
suggesting that homosexuality is an expression of self-
centeredness. Not only have my virtues changed to vices
because I'm gay, but also Sam believes I have "come out"
on purpose to spite the parish and my family. So it seems
that my choice is to be either deceitful (in the closet or
possibly half-in, half-out) or self-serving (out of the
closet). I am sick of this notion that being gay is the
equivalent of being selfish.

Bishop Estill also steadfastly denies that he knew of
my homosexuality before ordaining me to the priesthood.
For the longest time, I could not imagine why he would
persist in discrediting me, when in fact I had come out to
him as a gay man two weeks prior to my ordination. At
first, I thought he was just a poor listener, that he had
chosen not to hear me when, in the privacy of his office, I
spoke the words, "I'm gay," then proceeded to tell him
about my former homosexual relationships. Then, it
dawned on me that perhaps Bishop Estill felt obligated
professionally to deny that I had confessed my
homosexuality to him in order to honor the principle of
pastoral confidentiality. We priests are trained to forgive
and forget. Yet I had never asked Bishop Estill for
forgiveness, but rather, for equality and affirmation.

When the news broke, I began receiving obscene
phone calls and hate mail, much of it from clergy. One
anonymous caller called me a "cocksucking priest," and
my North Carolina colleagues accuse me of making a

travesty, a mockery of the priesthood. Here are some excerpts from their letters:

*

"I tried to warn you to proceed more slowly, to lay more groundwork before issuing a public statement about your homosexuality. Prudence and patience were part of Christ's own pattern. I thought for sure that you, as a musician, would have a better sense of timing. I'm disappointed in you, Zal."

*

"Your decision to write the *Witness* article was not only a lapse of better judgment, but also an outright act of insubordination toward your bishop and rector. You obviously have an unresolved authority conflict."

*

"In the interviews I have seen, you come across as a psychotic mess. My wish and prayer for you is that you will seek God's help and that of a psychiatrist or sex therapist in order that you might experience reorientation. I believe that by the grace of God, you could be successful in changing your feelings, thus learning to love and have sex with a woman. Living as a gay person, you will continue to be under the burden of sin, because you know homosexuality is not pleasing to the God whom you serve and represent. You've already lost your job. Now you must repent before you lose your life."

*

"You will, I hope, be charitable with those of us who can only be negative about what you've done. I admire your bravery and candor, but at the same time I can't help feeling that it may be too soon, and pastorally unwise, to be so completely open. Probably the biggest problem facing you is the nagging suspicion of some people, that as an openly gay priest, you must be cruising or 'on the make' during parish social hours. When you start mingling your personal desires with your professional conduct, the integrity of your priesthood suffers."

*

"By coming out as a gay man, you have become a 'one issue priest' and have therefore jeopardized the effectiveness of your ministry. Those called to the priesthood must display a breadth of interest and a potential to minister to a wide spectrum of the Church. None would gainsay your call to be a prophet, but in addition, you must be a reconciler and a pastor. How can you expect these qualities to be part of your priesthood when you insist on being such a strident activist?"

*

"You are a heretic and a disgrace to the profession. We Episcopal priests have always been the arbiters of good taste and decorum, but your *Witness* article was tasteless, immature and inappropriate to your task as a priest. I pray that you have learned your lesson from all this, and that in the future you will at least have the common decency to be asexual."

*

"I pray that in your pain, reconciliation is still uppermost in your mind. Have you spoken with your spiritual director of how best to be 'in peace and charity' with your sister, your former rector, and the bishop of North Carolina? Few things are more destructive to Christian living and ministry than the failure to forgive and the bearing of resentments, especially when you consider that they have been able to forgive you."

*

When Bishop Estill returned from General Convention where he had first read my *Witness* essay, he requested a meeting with me. At that meeting, he said that he had felt betrayed by the publication of my essay, and that he considered such a public disclosure of homosexuality to be "inappropriate behavior for a priest." He proceeded to tell me that my identification with the lesbian and gay community was also inappropriate. Stating that my priesthood was every bit as appropriate as his, I demanded that he accept me as his equal, i.e., a priest who has much to offer the Diocese of North Carolina. He refused. In a final effort to get at the root of his homophobia, I asked him to imagine kissing me, or making love with me, and he looked at me as if I were deranged, and said that he could easily revoke my license to function as a priest.

Bishop Estill kept saying how, although he could not support me as a priest, he wanted to be my "friend and pastor." He surrenders his capacity to minister to me because he has administrative control over parts of my life and ministry. How in the world can gay people ever be ministered to by religious homophobes when parts of our basic selves are denied, ridiculed, considered to be evil and needing to be exorcised, or even worse, hidden? The Church that demands us to lie, to be nice cuddly curates and not advocate gay rights, is one in need of purgation, love and forgiveness.

After meeting with Bishop Estill, I traveled with my youth group to the beach for a weekend retreat, during which I celebrated what I knew would probably be my final Eucharist with them. Normally, I participate in all recreational activities with them, but during this retreat, the teenagers noticed that I was remaining on the sidelines and urged me to join them. I held back, explaining that I wanted to watch them for a while. I can still picture each of them rejoicing in the sun, sand and surf, and how sad I felt because I realized I would soon lose them. While I sat on my blanket watching a touch football game, one of my teenage girls asked me to help her understand a particular scene in Sophocles' tragedy, *Antigone*, which she was reading for her high school English class (too bad you weren't around to help us). I noticed immediately how much the dialogue between Antigone and Creon resembled my recent meeting with the bishop, in that no meaningful communication took place. Creon's questions, like the bishop's, and Antigone's answers, like mine, are so inward, so absolute in their respective codes and visions of reality, that there is no exchange, no flexibility and no growth. Antigone is nauseated by Creon's avuncular, patronizing insistence on happiness, on the mundane routine which awaits her in married life. She flinches hysterically from domestic bliss, and elects to die for her convictions, unsullied by the unctuous compromises of bourgeois life. Let me share with you the power of her speech:

> I deemed it not the voice of Zeus that spake
> That herald's word, not yet did Justice, she
> Whose throne is beyond death, give such decree
> To hold among humanity. I did not rate
> Thy proclamations for a thing so great
> As by their human strength to have overtrod
> The unwritten and undying laws of God:
> Not of today nor yesterday, the same

Throughout all time they live; and whence they
    came
None knoweth. How should I through any fear
Of proud men dare to break them and then bear
God's judgment? — As for death, some day no
    doubt
I am sure to die. I knew that even without
Thy laws; and if I now shall die before
My time, that grace shall I be thankful for.
For one who lives ringed round by griefs, as I
Am living, is it not pure gain to die?
I tell thee, 'tis a trifling hurt or none
To die thus. Had I left my mother's son
Dead and unburied in that field to rot,
That would have hurt me. These things hurt me
    not,
Ye call this madness? Madness let it be,
For surely 'tis a madman judgeth me.
Why then delay? In all thy words to me
There is not — and God grant there never be! —
One word not hateful to me. I know too
To thee is hateful all that I hold true.
Yet, to see true, what praise could I have won
More high than to have saved my mother's son
From dogs and birds? — Aye, all these Elders
    here
Would praise me, were their lips not sealed by
    fear.
Oh, kings are fortunate; whate'er they please
They say unhindered; but no kings are these.

On Monday after the beach retreat, Ted stopped by
my office to tell me that he had heard that copies of my
Witness article were circulating around town.

"It's true," he said. "I've seen people reading it at the post office, at the A&P and at the gym. Two of your parishioners board their horses with us and both of them had read it."

An emergency vestry meeting was called Tuesday night during which Bishop Estill met for two-and-one-half hours with Sam and parish lay leaders. I was not permitted to attend the meeting, but was asked to wait in my office. At 10:30 p.m., the bishop left without acknowledging my presence, and Sam called me into the meeting room. The vestry began questioning me as if I were a criminal. Five of the twelve vestry members who had been aware of my homosexuality remained silent while the others proceeded to call me a liar and a heretic.

"What will the youth group think when they learn you're a homosexual?" one woman asked me. "Have you ever thought about that?"

I tried to answer their questions as calmly and completely as possible, and after a while, Sam issued me the following ultimatum:

"Zal, if we allow you to remain a priest on this staff, will you agree to stop all gay rights advocacy?"

I was stunned by his question. I didn't know how to respond. I wanted to work both at the parish and continue my writing, my work with AIDS patients, my involvement with Integrity. The pause seemed interminable, and Sam repeated his question. Finally I muttered, "I'm not sure," to which Sam responded, "Well, you better darn be sure," and when he said that, I was sure of only one thing, that I had no desire to continue working with this man.

I returned to my house late that night in a state of depression. I realized I would lose my Emmanuel friends.

To be alive, to be human, to create life, to commune with others as a priest, to know the depth of dialogue — and then suddenly to face only the dark, cold, quiet emptiness of floors and walls and ceilings. I was aware in the midst of the joy of creating a full life with my parishioners that one day it would end, that I would experience again feelings of isolation and loss. My body was quaking and I began to cry tears of defeat, panic and despair. I was still crying in the middle of my living room when I felt a hand touch my shoulder. One of my youth group advisors named Sally had been concerned about me, and stopped by late that night to check on me. She embraced me while I continued sobbing, helped me to bed, wiped the tears from my face with a warm washcloth and prayed with me.

I began telling friends and my parents that I would soon be leaving Emmanuel. On Friday, Sam requested my resignation to be effective on Monday. He had learned that an article on my *Witness* essay would appear in Sunday's *Raleigh News & Observer*.

"I'll still be able to celebrate the Eucharist on Sunday, won't I?" I asked. I had planned to preach on AIDS, using as my text 2 Corinthians 4:7-10: "But we have this treasure in earthen vessels, to show that the transcendent power belongs to God and not to us. We are afflicted in every way, but not crushed; perplexed but not driven to despair; persecuted, but not forsaken; struck down, but not destroyed; always carrying in the body the death of Jesus, so that the life of Jesus may also be manifested in our bodies."

"No," Sam replied. "I will not have the people of this parish come into church on Sunday morning and find a gay priest at the altar."

"Sam, why are you doing this to me?" I asked.

"Don't give me that line," he snapped. "I've tried to be understanding, but enough is enough. I can't trust you any longer. God only knows what you will be writing next. I want your resignation immediately."

And so I gave it to him, despite pleas from friends who wanted me to refuse to resign. In resigning, it was as if I had admitted that as a gay man, I was no longer qualified to serve as a priest at Emmanuel Church. Yet at that moment I was so afraid of Sam's fury, afraid of what he might do if I continued to resist, and so in a moment of weakness, naivete and defeat, I submitted my resignation.

"If only you and the parish would support me," I said. "It would have a great impact on the national Church."

"Well, you can just forget about that! People come here for solace, healing, comfort, a place to belong and to hear the Good News of Jesus Christ," he said. "We are not protestors. I will not have this parish aligned with a protest movement of any kind, especially one that concerns your homosexuality. I will not allow you to hurt or divide this parish. We're here to minister to the congregation, to help them become closer and nearer to God."

"What about me?" I asked. "Who plans to minister to me?"

"You should have thought about that before you wrote the *Witness* article," he said. "Run to your gay friends and let them minister to you. Your pain will only go away if you stop feeling sorry for yourself and begin ministering to others. For God's sake, Zal, stop and think what you're doing to yourself. What do you want to do to Christ's Church?"

Sam announced my resignation following all three
services that Sunday, the same morning a news story
appeared on the front page of the *News & Observer*. I was
present at the 11 a.m. service, during which I directed the
choir in music commemorating the feast of St. Michael
and All Angels.

In the days that followed, several television and radio
stations featured interviews with me. Parishioners
expressed their support for me through cards, letters and
phone calls. Mrs. Davis, the mother of Roger, who died of
AIDS, brought me meals each day and would sit with me
until I finished every bite.

Integrity responded in outrage and began mobilizing
and involving gay persons throughout the state. I began
receiving letters and phone calls from lesbians and gay
men who not only expressed their support, but also
needed a pastor with whom they could discuss various
issues. Bishop Estill met the other night with members of
the lesbian and gay community in response to the
Integrity statement. He refused to address any sections of
the statement, and stated succinctly that he would not
allow an avowed gay person to function as a priest in his
diocese. Although many lesbians and gay men eloquently
expressed our feelings of pain, exclusion and oppression
visited upon us by Church and society, we were unable to
persuade him to accept us in our total humanity, which
includes our demand that the Church recognizes and
affirms our relationships and our priestliness.

Gay speakers compared the current debate over
access to marriage and ordination to the 19th-century
debate over the availability of these sacraments to black
slaves. Noting that biblical justifications of slavery are
more plentiful than condemnations of homosexuality,

speakers asked that the Church not continue to sanction discrimination against gays as it previously supported racial prejudice and servitude. A black Baptist minister wrote me a letter that addresses this issue:

"At a time when racial prejudice has become a social taboo, bigotry aimed at gay persons has become quite vogue. And underlying this bigotry is ignorance devoid of compassion, understanding and tolerance. As a pastor of a black church, I am reminded of the civil rights struggles of many members of my congregation in the 1960s, and how gay persons are in the forefront of that same kind of struggle now. Many of them have relatives who were killed or maimed during that struggle, even as many gay persons fall victim to the mob ignorance of today. But you, my friend, are not dead, and while you have breath, you must continue the struggle."

Currently, I am struggling to keep at bay the inrush of doubt, despair, even regret. I know that a new Church is coming, a Church in which we can celebrate, sing, laugh and love freely; but at the moment, it is only a remote and fleeting awareness that does not stop the feelings of loneliness and grief.

Yet I'm not alone, but rather, surrounded by a cloud of witnesses. I'm staying with Ted and his lover at their farm in Southern Pines. Ted's lover, Gary, has taught me how to ride, and I'm a natural at shoveling manure, too. I take heart not only in my compassionate parishioners and gay friends who comfort and uphold me, but also in remembering that any genuinely inspired ministry by lesbians and gay men who are open about their sexuality is, in fact, a ministry of and for the whole people of God.

Each day comes and goes and I live in it as if it will last forever. For myself, there is no other way to live, to endure suffering and loneliness from lost relationships, while wondering how many more opportunities there will be for me to teach, to preach, to heal, to empower and to love. I'm trying to understand, Stephen, why you continue to believe that the Church needs "people like us." My gay friends urge me to leave the Church, to renounce my ministry, to stop devoting my life to an institution that has an uncanny ability to make gays feel like trash.

"You are practicing the ultimate in sado-masochism by remaining a priest in a denomination that pays a lot of lip service to inclusiveness, but fails to practice what it preaches," writes Mark from Vienna. I worry because, in the past, Mark has always been correct in his assessment of my personal life.

There is much work to be done, work that the Church is supposed to be doing, work that you and I are trained to do. I shall continue to practice my faith, to celebrate my experience of God within the context of a welcoming community, to join in solidarity with all oppressed persons, to cry out and take action against injustice, to empower persons who seek new ways to express spiritual truths in their lives. None of the preceding are possible, however, unless, as you have taught me, Stephen, we gay men and lesbians first learn to take care of ourselves and care for each other in our relationships.

I shall close this letter with yet another excerpt from a letter sent to me by a member of the parish's singles group:

"As a practicing heterosexual woman, I have had highs and lows in personal relationships. Having been divorced for twelve years, I am facing the painful truth of being single and not having children. Wanting marriage, a family and membership in a country club does not cause those things to exist.

"So, like you, I also live on the margins of life, on the edge of society in which I cannot be completely accepted. Through your witness, you have given me permission to be alone and sometimes lonely. You have also given me the strength to look for God in the margins and to see Christ in places I never believed imaginable."

With my love,
Zal

postscript

On Ash Wednesday, 1986, Zal Sherwood moved from North Carolina to Santa Fe, New Mexico. He worked as a gardener and waiter while undergoing a period of what he describes as 'ecclesiastical detoxification.'

In July, 1986, Sherwood was granted canonical residence by the Rt. Rev. H. Coleman McGehee, Jr., Bishop of Michigan. He currently works as an assistant priest at St. Paul's Church, Jackson, Michigan, and as a chaplain at the nearby Southern Michigan State Prison.

Other books of interest from
ALYSON PUBLICATIONS

Don't miss our FREE BOOK offer at the end of this section.

☐ **SEX POSITIVE,** by Larry Uhrig, $7.00. Many of today's religious leaders condemn homosexuality, distorting Biblical passages to support their claims. But spirituality and sexuality are closely linked, writes Uhrig, and he explores the positive Biblical foundations for gay relationships.

☐ **THE TWO OF US,** by Larry Uhrig, $7.00. The author draws on his years of counseling with gay people to give some down-to-earth advice about what makes a relationship work. He gives special emphasis to the religious aspects of gay unions.

☐ **THE LAVENDER COUCH,** by Marny Hall, $8.00. Here is a guide to the questions that should be considered by lesbians or gay men considering therapy or already in it: How do you choose a good therapist? What kind of therapy is right for you? When is it time to leave therapy?

☐ **REFLECTIONS OF A ROCK LOBSTER: A story about growing up gay,** by Aaron Fricke, $6.00. When Aaron Fricke took a male date to the senior prom, no one was surprised: he'd gone to court to be able to do so, and the case had made national news. Here Aaron tells his story, and shows what gay pride can mean in a small New England town.

☐ **SOCRATES, PLATO AND GUYS LIKE ME: Confessions of a gay schoolteacher,** by Eric Rofes, $7.00. When Eric Rofes began teaching sixth grade at a conservative private school, he soon felt the strain of a split identity. Here he describes his two years of teaching from within the closet, and his difficult decision to finally come out.

☐ **TALK BACK! A gay person's guide to media action,** $4.00. When were you last outraged by prejudiced media coverage of gay people? Chances are it hasn't been long. This short, highly readable book tells how you, in surprisingly little time, can do something about it.

☐ **DEAR SAMMY: Letters from Gertrude Stein and Alice B. Toklas,** by Samuel M. Steward, $8.00. As a young man, Samuel M. Steward journeyed to France to meet the two women he so admired. It was the beginning of a long friendship. Here he combines his fascinating memoirs of Toklas and Stein with photos and more than a hundred of their letters.

☐ **A HISTORY OF SHADOWS,** by Robert C. Reinhart, $7.00. A fascinating look at gay life during the Depression, the war years, the McCarthy witchhunts, and the sixties — through the eyes of four men who were friends during those forty years.

☐ **THE MEN WITH THE PINK TRIANGLE,** by Heinz Heger, $6.00. In a chapter of gay history that is only recently coming to light, thousands of homosexuals were thrown into the Nazi concentration camps along with Jews and others who failed to fit the Aryan ideal. There they were forced to wear a pink triangle so that they could be singled out for special abuse. Most perished. Heger is the only one ever to have told his full story.

Get this book free!

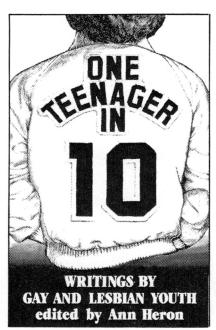

Twenty-eight young people, most of high school age, share their coming-out experiences in *One Teenager in Ten.* Editor Ann Heron has selected accounts from all over the United States and Canada in which gay young people tell how they dealt with feeling different, telling parents and friends, and learning to like themselves.

If you order at least three other books from us, you may request a FREE copy of this important book. (See order form on next page.)

To get these books:

Ask at your favorite bookstore for the books listed here. You may also order by mail. Just fill out the coupon below, or use your own paper if you prefer not to cut up this book.

GET A FREE BOOK! When you order any three books listed here at the regular price, you may request a *free* copy of *One Teenager in Ten*

— — — — — — — — — — — — — — — — —

Enclosed is $_____ for the following books. (Add $1.00 postage when ordering just one book; if you order two or more, we'll pay the postage.)

1. _____
2. _____
3. _____
4. _____
5. _____

☐ Send a free copy of *One Teenager in Ten* as offered above. I have ordered at least three other books.

name: _____

address: _____

city: _____ state: _____ zip: _____

ALYSON PUBLICATIONS
Dept. H-2, 40 Plympton St., Boston, Mass. 02118

This offer expires April 30, 1989. After that date, please write for current catalog.